SPEAKING HATEFULLY

RHETORIC AND **DEMOCRATIC** DELIBERATION

VOLUME 6

EDITED BY CHERYL GLENN AND J. MICHAEL HOGAN
THE PENNSYLVANIA STATE UNIVERSITY

Editorial Board:

Rhetoric and Democratic Deliberation is a series of groundbreaking monographs and edited volumes focusing on the character and quality of public discourse in politics and culture. It is sponsored by the Center for Democratic Deliberation, an interdisciplinary center for research, teaching, and outreach on issues of rhetoric, civic engagement, and public deliberation.

Other books in the series:

SPEAKING HATEFULLY

CULTURE, COMMUNICATION, AND POLITICAL ACTION
IN HUNGARY

DAVID BOROMISZA-HABASHI

The Pennsylvania State University Press | University Park, Pennsylvania

Library of Congress Cataloging-in-Publication Data

Boromisza-Habashi, David.
    Speaking hatefully : culture, communication,
    and political action in Hungary / David
    Boromisza-Habashi.
        p.   cm. — (Rhetoric and democratic
    deliberation)
Includes bibliographical references and index.
Summary: "An empirical study of hate speech in
Hungary, examining the cultural foundations of
public communication and how cultural thinking
can be used to inform political action through public
expression"—Provided by publisher.
ISBN 978-0-271-05637-1 (cloth : alk. paper)
ISBN 978-0-271-05638-8 (pbk. : alk. paper)
1. Hate speech—Hungary.
2. Oral communication—Social aspects—Hungary.
I. Title.

P95.54.B67   2013
302.2'24209439—dc23
2012028140

The Pennsylvania State University Press is a member
of the Association of American University Presses.

It is the policy of The Pennsylvania State University
Press to use acid-free paper. Publications on uncoated
stock satisfy the minimum requirements of American
National Standard for Information Sciences—
Permanence of Paper for Printed Library Material,
ANSI Z39.48–1992.

To my families

CONTENTS

ACKNOWLEDGMENTS

My work on hate speech was inspired by four families, all of which I call mine. My first family was the one I had grown up in: a conservative, Christian, middle-class, white family in Hungary. Some members of this family held many strong convictions and had only few curious questions about the racial, ethic, and political composition of Hungarian society. My second family consisted of me and my father's Hungarian friend Gyurka (the eminent pathologist Dr. George K. Nagy of Albany, New York), a true humanist who acted as my moral and intellectual father during some of my formative years in the United States of America. Gyurka taught me to see people where my first family saw only social categories. Then, there was my third family, my wife Nora's family in Egypt. This family of mostly progressive Coptic Christians, living in a predominantly conservative Muslim society, helped me develop a keen sense of the minority experience. It is this sense that helps Nora, me, and our two daughters, my fourth family, understand and appreciate our experiences of life in the United States.

Standing at the intersection of these four families I sometimes find myself asking uncomfortable questions: Were those members of my first family who talked dismissively about the Roma, Jews, Chinese immigrants, alleged communists, and the poor speaking hate speech? Do adjectives like "hateful" or "racist" apply to them based on the way they talked? What types of social, moral, and political relations are talked into being once we decide either to apply these adjectives to one another or to withhold them? And, generally speaking, where does the morally based criticism of others' communicative conduct, or the withholding of such criticism, take the critic and those critiqued?

This book is an exploration of what is at stake—socially, morally, and politically—when one asks and answers such questions in a particular cultural community.

Speaking Hatefully bears the marks of many discussions with colleagues and friends. I am indebted first to Donal Carbaugh, who guided the dissertation that served as the foundation of this book. I benefited greatly from conversations with colleagues in the Department of Communication at the University of Colorado, Boulder, especially Bob Craig, John Jackson, Pete Simonson, and Karen Tracy. I owe thanks to many others who discussed my research with me or commented on earlier versions of chapters over the years, especially Mike Agar, Brenda Allen, Michael Ash, Benjamin Bailey, Michael Berry, János Boromisza, Richard Buttny, Vernon Cronen, Matt D'Aprile, Miklós Ercsényi, John Gastil, Krista Harper, Tamar Katriel, Steph Kent, Derek Miller, László Munteán, Gerry Philipsen, Lisa Rudnick, Béla Runtág, David Seibold, Robin Shoaps, Razvan Sibii, Leah Sprain, Rebecca Townsend, and Kwesi Yankah. I am grateful to the Hungarian Scholars' Club of Massachusetts for inviting me to present my work at the Massachusetts Institute of Technology in 2006. I also thank those directly involved in moving this book through the publication process: Kendra Boileau, editor in chief at Penn State University Press, series editors Mike Hogan and Cheryl Glenn, and two anonymous reviewers.

I would like to thank the College of Arts and Sciences at the University of Colorado, Boulder, for supporting the publication of this book with a generous Kayden Research Grant.

Two of the chapters in the book are based on previously published articles. An earlier version of chapter 4 was published as "Freedom of Expression, Hate Speech, and Models of Personhood in Hungarian Political Discourse" in *Communication Law Review* 7, no. 1 (2007). Chapter 5 is based on an article that appeared in *Text and Talk* 31, no. 1 (2011), published by de Gruyter and available at http://www.degruyter.com. Permission to reprint the two political cartoons in chapter 1 was given by the artist, Marabu. I thank István Boromisza for helping me obtain this permission.

INTRODUCTION:
CULTURAL THINKING ABOUT SOCIAL ISSUES

"Hate speech" is a social issue. There is no consensus about what the concept "hate speech" means. "Hate speech" is a term that points to a type of public expression. "Hate speech" is *gyűlöletbeszéd* in Hungarian.

This book investigates the relationships among these propositions, and asks what we can learn from those relationships. More generally speaking, this book is about the cultural foundations of public communication, and about how cultural thinking can be used to inform political action through public expression. My goal is to demonstrate to my readers—scholars and students interested in a cultural approach to public expression, political actors who wish to understand issues in their full complexity before they act, and others—that public communication and political action never happen in a cultural vacuum. The book is also an ethnographic study of the public life of the term "hate speech" (*gyűlöletbeszéd*, pronounced roughly as dyoo-lo-let-beh-sayd) in Hungary during the heyday of the hate speech debates between 2000 and 2006.

As an ethnographer interested in public discourse, I have been observing the work of policy makers and political activists in the United States and Europe since 2004. I noticed that their admirable efforts seem to run into two common obstacles: although most people in their communities agree that hate speech is a social evil, there is only limited consensus about what constitutes hate speech and what should be done about it. I believe these obstacles can be best understood and addressed at the point where culture, public communication, and political action intersect.

Does this lack of consensus render political action impossible or pointless? Hardly. Political actors engage in productive political action every day in the name of hotly contested political concepts such as abortion, terrorism, or discrimination. Contestation seems to frustrate political action designed to address social issues when those who engage in political action do not recognize, or outright deny, that the concepts in the name of which they engage in political battles are indeed contested. Political actors who do not confront the contested nature of the concepts around which they organize their agendas tend to find themselves locked in endless confrontations over the "correct" definitions of elusive terms like democracy, fascism, or poverty. The meaning of hate speech has also been the subject of many hours and days of fruitless political wrangling in books, state institutions, and political campaigns. We hear the same questions repeated from country to country, from year to year: What groups can become the targets of hate speech? Can a member of an ethnic minority speak hate speech against the majority society? What particular utterances count as hate speech? Should a list of such utterances be created? Does it matter whether speakers of hate speech actually hate their targets? How, if at all, does hate speech injure the target? Is hate speech talk or action? If it is action, is it criminal action sanctionable by law?

Cultural Thinking and Analysis

The quotation marks I occasionally attach to the term "hate speech" are a visual reminder that the term is not a simple window on reality. It is not to be regarded a transparent concept that we can glance through and see the sharp image of a pressing social issue. The quotation marks highlight a commitment to cultural thinking about hate speech that requires a careful examination of various local meanings of the term active in particular communities of speakers. My objective in this book is to introduce readers to a cultural mode of thinking they can use to explore these meanings and new types of creative, culturally informed political action by reflecting on the cultural foundations of public talk about social issues. A related objective is to illustrate how culture and political action are linked through, and interact in, public communication.

Cultural thinking about contested political concepts such as hate speech compels one to adopt a few basic assumptions. First, *the meanings of political concepts can shape the meanings of the issues for which they stand.* For example, in chapter 3 of this book I show how, in the context of a particular media event, the interpretation of *gyűlöletbeszéd* as a type of content led some Hungarians to worry about racism, and how their opponents, who interpreted *gyűlöletbeszéd* as a type of tone expressed concern about the vitriolic style of Hungarian public discourse. What follows from this assumption is that changing the meaning of a political concept can change the interpretation of the issue for which it stands.

Second, *political concepts, and the issues they stand for, are the elements of language use.* Our most sacred political ideals (such as equality, justice, or democratic participation) and the social evils we are concerned about (such as hate speech, discrimination, or poverty) exist in large part because people talk about them in the streets, in parliaments and courts around the world, and write newspaper articles, books, movies, and plays about them.[1] The meanings of our political concepts and of the issues they denote are born, live, and die in language use. If we want to understand why political concepts and issues matter to people, and how people can be influenced to think and act differently about them, we must pay careful attention to how they are used.

Third, *the contestation of political concepts is morally infused action.* Simply put, people contest the meaning of political concepts because they care. Determining the meaning of hate speech is not an exercise in lexicography for many, but a matter of clean conscience and human dignity. This observation applies, as we will see in chapter 5, even to those who deny that hate speech is a type of observable public expression and are convinced that the whole hate speech agenda is a clever political ploy designed to silence certain types of political speech.

Fourth, cultural thinking requires us to accept that *contestation involves the clash of equally coherent (although not equally acceptable) cultural logics.* For a political actor to claim, in knee-jerk fashion, that one interpretation of a widely contested term like hate speech is wrongheaded or incoherent is to avoid cultural thinking. Political actors can benefit from carefully considering talk about social issues in groups whose political actions or stances they wish to change. For example, unfamiliar or downright strange ways of using political concepts can function as a window on alternative moral systems or cultural logics that serve as the motor of political action in a political group or constituency. Cultural thinking, in sum, can be used to form and extend political coalitions and pave the way toward joint action.

Finally, *understanding competing cultural logics is a critical element of creative political action.* The existence of multiple, partially overlapping, and partially incompatible cultural logics is a fact of life in multicultural societies. A cultural orientation toward these logics is a necessary political response to contemporary social reality. It is also a key element of political creativity—that is, the ability to gather elements of familiar political talk and recombine them into unfamiliar, intriguing, and persuasive forms of expression.

The view of culture I am adopting in this book is not the traditional view that sees culture as something exotic peoples have. I invite readers to think about culture not as a possession but as a way of looking at the everyday practices of a people they have trouble understanding, due to a lack of familiarity with the people themselves, their everyday lives, their language, or their history. Cultural thinking is preceded by a decision that one makes consciously or unconsciously, to always give a social (or political) group the benefit of the doubt. The decision requires the cultural observer to adopt the working assumption that there must be a way in which the seemingly exotic practices of the observed group make perfectly good common sense, and that the group's common sense may not be identical with that of the observer. Observers using cultural thinking should also prepare themselves for the possibility that those practices of the observed group that seem to make immediate sense to the observer have an entirely different meaning from the perspective of the group.

Cultural thinking, however, is only the start. The assumptions listed above must be translated into analysis. This book demonstrates how that can be done.

"Hate Speech"

The difference between the cultural approach to hate speech and political action I am offering in this book and other influential scholarly work on the subject is that existing studies regard hate speech as a transparent concept that stands for a kind of talk with describable characteristics. Simply put, for the vast majority of scholars, hate speech is a distinct object with a singular meaning available for description and evaluation. In his groundbreaking book *The Nature of Prejudice*, the social psychologist Gordon Allport regards hate speech—or, as he calls it, antilocution—as the manifestation of an individual's ethnic prejudice and as the first step toward violence.[2] In *Excitable Speech*, the philosopher Judith Butler interrogates the source of the power of hate speech to injure its targets, and finds that source in linguistic performance.[3] The linguist Robin Lakoff criticizes those who regard all forms of public speech free speech for denying that hate speech successfully fuses words with injurious action.[4] In a similar manner, critical race theorists condemn free speech absolutists for turning a blind eye toward speech that causes actual harm to actual people.[5] Discourse analysts warn that although we see fewer and fewer instances of outright racist and discriminatory expression, more subtle forms of hate speech continue to reproduce hierarchical social relations among racial and ethnic groups in Western societies.[6] The work of these scholars shares the notion that hate speech is expression that consists of words, and that words powerfully shape social relations.

We learn little from this type of work about how hate speech itself had become an issue that people in Western societies started to pay attention to in the twentieth century. How did hate speech become an object of concern, one may ask, and how are notions about its existence and characteristics cultivated (or questioned) in contemporary Western democracies? The legal scholar Samuel Walker devoted an entire book to the question of why there are no laws restricting hate speech in the United States despite a long tradition of civil rights struggles.[7] At first blush, the situation is indeed perplexing. If civil rights movements were able to inspire concern about hate speech in the American public, why did the country's legal system not respond by creating appropriate sanctions against it? Walker says that the strong American commitment to free expression does not by itself resolve the conundrum. His theory of the lack of legal sanctions against hate speech in the United States "is fairly simple: ideas have no force in the world without advocates. Regardless of the merits of a particular idea, it has little practical effect without a person or organization to persuade others to support it, to bring and argue cases before courts of law, to propose legislation, and eventually to transform the idea into public policy."[8] The American Civil Liberties Union championed the protection of the First Amendment, the National Association for the Advancement of Colored People stood up for the Fourteenth; the idea of imposing restrictions on hate speech and other kinds of offensive speech (such as Holocaust denial) did not have enough supporters in the United States. In Germany, France, Israel, Poland, and the Czech Republic, among other countries, it did.

Walker's point is important from the perspective of the cultural thinking for which I am arguing. Social issues do not sustain their own significance; their degree of poignancy depends on the actions of politically and morally committed people. One significant aspect of such action is how we name and talk about our social issues.

The term "hate speech" does not only point to certain forms of public communication—it *is* an element of public communication. As such, its meaning lives in its everyday use, and that use is shaped by various, often competing, cultural logics and norms, even within societies that share the same language. To capture the complicated cultural life of hate speech, I reverse the course of existing research on the subject. Instead of proceeding from meaning toward doing (identifying the meaning of hate speech, and then locating examples of it in society), I proceed from doing to meaning (identifying examples of the public use of the term hate speech and then mapping its many local meanings).

As I discovered in the course of an ethnographic field study I conducted between 2004 and 2007 in Hungary, *gyűlöletbeszéd* can attain a life of its own. One night in early 2004 I was having dinner and drinks with some old friends in a restaurant in downtown Budapest. Multiple conversations were going on across the table, and one caught my attention. My friend Miki, a young Hungarian architect with a passion for Bauhaus, good beer, and the great outdoors, was explaining in a heated, bitter tone how he was "fed up" with *gyűlöletbeszéd*. I e-mailed him the next day and asked him what he meant. His disgruntled response came back fast: "I am not fed up with *gyűlöletbeszéd* itself, I am fed up with the word. Technically, it's meaningless, its meaning can't be defined, but all dumbass journalists throw it around constantly. By the way, you can't definitely say that about any kind of talk [i.e., that it is hate speech] because the speaker and their captive audience would obviously disagree—to them, it is a natural feeling. The question is where we look at it from, on which side we stand." Intrigued, I asked him what he meant by talk being a result of a "natural feeling." He replied, "The zealous listeners of someone who expresses hatred for others will not describe that talk as incitement to hatred because they are already hateful . . ., they simply went to hear a like-minded speaker."

It took me a long time to fully appreciate the cultural meaningfulness of Miki's remarks. For many Hungarians, *gyűlöletbeszéd* is a problem of political and moral affiliation. The act of charging a public speaker with hate speech is much more than an act of description—it involves taking sides. The charge also posits an irreconcilable difference of opinion between the speaker evaluating another speaker's talk as hate speech, and the alleged speaker of hate speech and their captive audience. Under no circumstances will a speaker (or their audience) agree that the utterances in question qualify as hate speech. The charge of hate speech inevitably comes from an external party, and it prompts disagreement with the same inevitability.

Miki's remarks take us to the heart of the argument I develop in the following chapters. From a cultural perspective on communication, hate speech exists in a process of social interaction among three kinds of participants: alleged perpetrators (who are criticized for having performed hate speech), targets (who are in the position to be offended by hate speech), and judges (who link perpetrators' utterances to the term "hate speech" and propose sanctions). This rather commonsensical observation has an important cultural implication: whether what someone says publicly *counts as* hate speech depends on not one but three parties, who will never agree. Alleged perpetrators will resist the judge's judgment, judges will often use the perpetrator's resistance as evidence of their guilt, and targets may or may not support the judge in their quest for social justice or political gain. (In fact, very often they are quite content being quiet observers.) The charge of hate speech is an act of evaluation, and evaluation implies not only a definition of hate speech but a moral stance as well. Where moral systems clash, definitions of morally charged political concepts are likely to abound.

Surveying the Cultural Terrain of Public Communication

Scholarly works with ethnographic interest in Hungarian public discourse are rare. The majority of scholarly work in Hungary concerned with communication as a social phenomenon is heavily theoretical and quantitative.[9] The work closest to my area of research is done at the Hungarian Academy of Sciences in the Center for Political Discourse Studies (CEPODS) where a group of scholars pursues compelling empirical analyses of Hungarian political phenomena such as civic radicalism,[10] the discourses of the "political alien,"[11] and of the right-wing conservative party Fidesz,[12] among others. However, the scholars affiliated with the institute do not adopt a cultural view of public discourse.

As any ethnographer worth his or her salt would do, throughout my fieldwork in Hungary I followed the two basic principles of ethnography formulated by the anthropologist Mike Agar.[13] First, I sought to identify cultural patterns in hate speech–related Hungarian communicative practices. To borrow a term from the father of the ethnography of communication, the late Dell Hymes, I was looking for ways of speaking associated with *gyűlöletbeszéd*.[14] The notion of ways of speaking links observable communicative patterns to particular elements of their social context, such as physical setting, participants, their interactional goals, and the type of communicative event.[15] The findings presented in this book detail the fundamental observation that certain kinds of people with certain moral and intellectual convictions can be expected to talk about hate speech in certain ways within a community of speakers. Second, the search for patterns in Hungary made it necessary to adopt the learning role of the student/child/apprentice in relation to Hungarian public talk. I attended public lectures organized by the Hungarian chapter of Blood and Honor, a pro-Nazi group, and the annual gathering of antifascists with the same desire to learn various cultural logics of public discourse. Before my reader accuses me of moral relativism, a charge frequently leveled at ethnographers, I hasten to add that the desire to learn and the desire to follow are two very different kinds of intellectual and moral impulse. The willingness to learn is best understood as a "working morality" on the part of the ethnographer—my personal moral stance toward hate speech will be elaborated in chapter 6. Readers with further interest in the theoretical and methodological underpinnings of the work presented in this book can turn to the appendix.

The goal of ethnography is to generate cultural knowledge; the goal of political action is to influence others' conduct. What can someone interested or invested in political action learn from an ethnography of a concept? From one perspective, the contribution of ethnography to political action and advocacy is modest. An ethnography cannot tell political actors what to do about a social issue, simply because most ethnographers lack expertise in designing political action or policy that target social change. Most ethnographers, with the exception of a notable few, work in academic environments. Professional life in an academic department inspires plenty of locally relevant political action, but involvement in such action rarely prepares ethnographers to produce ethnographies capable of directly shaping political action. Ethnographers, however, are well prepared to explain how members of a social group believe the world works and how it should work. I describe and analyze the use of the concept "hate speech" in a particular setting—Hungary—at a particular historical moment—a decade and a half after the end of communist rule. Metaphorically speaking, I want to offer political actors a way of mapping the political landscape they are attempting to conquer. This map will have little to say about the number and size of political groups, their sources of funding, or the details of their political agendas. It will, however, have much to say about the political and social significance of *gyűlöletbeszéd* as a communicative resource for political action.

At a higher level of abstraction, this book may intrigue readers interested in the cultural logic of political action. This group of readers is likely to include intellectuals and political practitioners seeking to critically examine dominant ways of talking about pressing social issues, or who feel a need to understand social issues from *all* stakeholders' perspectives. Using the case of hate speech in Hungary, the following chapters demonstrate how communication becomes the site where political action becomes related to, or grounded in, culture. More particularly, the book highlights four ways that public communication about social issues is founded on culture: through the (historical, economic, political, etc.) *contexts* communal members identify as relevant, the diversity of *meanings* (what meanings *gyűlöletbeszéd* has), competing *interpretations* (how public actors arrive at and promote a set of meanings over others), and competing *moral systems* (what norms inform public speech, and what cultural beliefs inform those values).

Why Hungary?

The question is perfectly legitimate; after all, most readers of this book are likely to reside in the English-speaking part of the world, where hate speech has been a concern for at least two decades, particularly in the United States. Why not discuss the ongoing debate about the issue in the United States instead? After all, there can be no doubt that the debate over hate speech was, and continues to be, culturally significant. One only has to think of the campus speech codes controversy of the 1990s,[16] or the recent legal case the father of the late U.S. Marine Lance Corporal Matthew A. Snyder brought against Westboro Baptist Church. U.S. debates, obviously, have cultural foundations of their own.

As ethnographers are fond of saying, ethnography makes the familiar strange and the strange familiar. I intend to make hate speech strange by locating it in a non-English-speaking cultural community and then making it familiar again by explaining the cultural logic motivating its use. We naturally tend to respond to social issues and controversies in our own communities by taking sides. We feel that these issues directly concern us as communal members, and therefore we feel compelled to adopt a position on the issue. Rushing to declare a position on an issue, however, undermines cultural thinking, which requires carefully listening to all members of a community of speakers. An influential advocate of cultural thinking, the anthropologist Clifford Geertz, reflected on the contribution of cultural anthropology to the world in this way: "It is from the . . . difficult achievement of seeing ourselves amongst others, as a local example of the forms human life has locally taken, a case among cases, a world among worlds, that the largeness of mind, without which objectivity is self-congratulation and tolerance a sham, comes."[17] Cultural interpretation, the practice of making sense of unfamiliar systems of meaning from the perspective of the people who rely on those systems for conducting their day-to-day lives, is a powerful mode of representation because it opens up the interplay of cultural differences and similarities to the reader.[18] The ethnographic study of *gyűlöletbeszéd* in Hungary presented in this book is intended to provide precisely this type of intellectual experience. I am counting on my readers' familiarity with hate speech as a social issue, and, at the same time, I am counting on their lack of familiarity with how the issue is meaningful in the Hungarian cultural context. It is in this tension between familiarity and the lack thereof, between the recognition of similarity and difference, where cultural thinking finds its inspiration. My hope is that this book will generate such inspiration, and that this inspiration will prompt some of my readers to rethink political action through public talk against hate speech in their own societies.

Structure of the Book

Chapter 1 provides the reader with a brief sketch of the troubled sociocultural context in which Hungarian public talk about hate speech occurs. The legal history of hate speech and its related terms shows that these took on special significance at times when Hungary entered a state of liminality, or sociocultural transition. I also offer a brief overview of a particular legal case (commonly referred to as the Hegedűs affair) with an allegation of hate speech at its center. One intended outcome of this chapter is to help the reader make the first step toward cultural thinking, the temporary suspension of the commonly held interpretation of hate speech as racist or sexist talk. Another goal is to create an opportunity for non-Hungarian readers to regard Hungarian hate speech as a term that acquires specific types of meanings in its particular cultural context.

Chapter 2 documents various competing meanings of hate speech active in the Hungarian context. I distinguish act-, event-, and style-level cultural interpretations of terms for communicative action to capture these meanings. Act-level interpretations make sense of hate speech as the act of an individual actor; event-level interpretations present hate speech as public communication involving a number of actors; style-level interpretations present a speaker's use of hate speech as the outcome of a choice among various related forms of expression. In this chapter, I further elaborate the cultural model of hate speech as the result of an interaction among perpetrators, targets, and judges.

In chapter 3 I demonstrate the clash between two dominant interpretive strategies Hungarian speakers use as they identify acts of *gyűlöletbeszéd*. Proponents of the tone-based interpretation argue that one can tell hate speech by the hateful tone or style of public expression. In contrast, the content-based interpretation seeks to identify particular kinds of content as tokens of hate speech, such as racist utterances or Holocaust denial. The chapter is a study of a media event that began with a radio broadcast on the Budapest radio station Klub Rádió on September 2, 2004, and ended with the publication of the last of eleven articles in the Hungarian political and literary weekly *Élet és Irodalom* (Life and literature).

Chapter 4 shifts attention from various interpretations of hate speech to Hungarian politicians' views of sanctions against it. In 2003, at the height of the hate speech controversy, three parliamentary standing committees were tasked with evaluating a controversial bill designed to revise the Hungarian criminal code and to turn hate speech into a criminal act. All MPs speaking at the meetings regarded hate speech as despicable but they disagreed vehemently about the value of legal sanctions. In this chapter I show that MPs' opposing beliefs about the nature of a legally constituted person explains, at least in part, why they reached opposing conclusions about the bill.

The main concern of chapter 5 is political resistance. There are speakers on the Hungarian political scene who claim to detect hidden political agendas in dominant antiracist political talk about *gyűlöletbeszéd*. The chapter reconstructs four arguments against what I refer to as the hate speech agenda: that it is founded on the deliberate corruption of the Hungarian language; that it reveals that antiracists are pursuing an alien political utopia; that it is fraught with ideological inconsistency; and that antiracist proponents of the hate speech agenda are themselves filled with hatred. I also describe the underlying moral system that lends coherence to these arguments.

In the concluding chapter I discuss the possibility of using cultural knowledge to inform political action carried out through public expression. Cultural knowledge is available to the practitioner in three forms: as information, as counsel, and as a symbolic template for creative action. The chapters preceding chapter 6 are devoted to presenting cultural knowledge as information. In this chapter I develop particular recommendations for Hungarian public speakers who speak what I call the language of unity. Two locally relevant ways of authoring unity are discussed: the use of rhetoric and proposals for "dialogue" among relevant state or media institutions. The chapter ends with a call on practitioners to use local symbolic resources to design creative political action against derogatory public talk targeting historically disadvantaged minorities.

My reader may wonder about the extent to which the ethnographic findings presented in this book hold true today. Those who attempt to represent the ever-changing cultural life of a community are shooting at a moving target. I cannot guarantee that what I had learned about "hate speech" between 2004 and 2007 will apply to other cultural contexts, or that my findings and claims will fully explain the significance of derogatory talk about minorities and immigrants in today's Hungarian public talk. Nevertheless, it is my hope that those who read this book will walk away from it convinced that culture and political action are related through communication, and that culturally informed political action is a promising possibility.

I

HISTORY AS CONTEXT

Issues do not just "lie there," waiting to be discussed—they are the products of communication.[1] The communicative "making" of issues, as a type of social action, always takes place in, and draws on, a variety of contexts. The first element of cultural thinking about a social issue like hate speech is the careful examination of those (historical, geographic, and political) contexts in which the issue at hand had taken shape. To that end, this chapter explores a context Hungarians saw and discussed as particularly relevant to the issue: history.

Hungary: A Liminal State

Situated in the former geopolitical buffer zone between the Cold War East and the West, Hungary was among the countries that quickly made the transition from state censorship on public expression to complete freedom of expression, press, and religion after the fall of communism in 1989. Today, the ten-million-strong, thousand-year-old country has a democratically elected government, it is a member of such international organizations as the European Union, NATO, and the United Nations, and it is busily transforming the remnants of its former planned economic system into a market economy.

Since a good portion of Hungarian public speaking is done in politics and the media, a few words of introduction about the current Hungarian political system and the media are in order. In 1989, Hungary adopted a Westminster-style parliamentary system featuring all elements of the British model except its bicameral structure. Hungary has a head of state (the President of the Republic), a head of government (the Prime Minister), and a multiparty political system. In the 2010 parliamentary elections, four parties won seats in the unicameral, 386-member National Assembly. During the first two decades of the new democratic state, two main political power blocks emerged. The conservative right is dominated by Fidesz–Hungarian Civic Union (Fidesz–MPP); the largest and most influential political player on the left is the Hungarian Socialist Party (MSZP). The political influence of other political parties arranged along the Hungarian political spectrum—communists, liberals, radical conservatives, and the far right—ebbs and flows.

Since I relied heavily on media discourse in my ethnographic work, let us briefly survey the contemporary Hungarian media landscape at the start of the twenty-first century. There were five television channels with national coverage in the country. Three of these channels (M1, M2, Duna TV) were state-funded public broadcasting services, and the other two (RTL Klub, TV2) were commercial enterprises. Approximately 220 commercial television channels and 30 privately owned radio stations existed in the country. Only three state-funded radio stations (Kossuth, Bartók, Petőfi) had national coverage. The Hungarian equivalent of the Federal Communications Commission in the United States is the National Radio and Television Commission. In the year 2000, the number of registered print media reached 1,600. The circulation of two daily newspapers (*Népszabadság, Metro*) exceeded two hundred thousand copies; the number of other major national newspapers reached roughly fifteen thousand each.[2]

Existing ethnographies of Hungarian public discourse concur that Hungary's public sphere had been, and continues to be, shaped by frequent and drastic shifts and tensions in the country's political, economic, social, and geographic landscape.[3] In Hungary, it is something of a cultural commonplace to say that, during the past century, the country's political systems ranged from dual monarchy (Austro-Hungarian monarchy) to national socialism (Nazism), from state socialism (communism) to Western-style liberal democracy. In addition, migration and the country's shifting borders often led to tense interethnic relations between the dominant Hungarian group (Magyars) and other ethnic groups. Today, the Hungarian state officially recognizes thirteen ethnic minorities (Bulgarian, Roma, Greek, Croatian, Polish, German, Armenian, Romanian, Ruthenian, Serbian, Slovak, Slovenian, and Ukrainian). Although not officially registered as "national minorities," politically, culturally, and economically influential Jewish and Chinese communities exist in the country as well. The size and political influence of these minority groups vary, but in relation to the majority Hungarian (Magyar) society the number of self-ascribed members of minorities is small (roughly 3 percent of the population). A vast range of scholarly work chronicles numerous manifestations of anti-Semitism[4] and anti-Romani sentiment[5] in Hungary's history.

The most recent transition from state socialism to capitalist democracy led the noted Hungarian cultural critic Elemér Hankiss to describe Hungary as existing in a state of perpetual liminality or "in-betweenness."[6] Hankiss notes that the fall of communism in 1989 did not bring independence for Hungary; rather, the country simply shifted the direction of its dependence from the former Soviet bloc toward the European Union, NATO, the World Bank, the International Monetary Fund, and Wall Street. Hankiss borrows the analytic term liminality from anthropologist Victor Turner[7] to argue that Hungary, caught in the throes of transition from one sociopolitical structure to the next, experiences the sociocultural chaos Turner associates with liminal states in traditional societies. Hankiss reviews a variety of ways in which Hungarians make sense of the transition in public discourse and concludes that, unfortunately, these sense-making strategies add up to a negative kind of liminality that works against the formation of creative, visionary social groups (collectives that Turner refers to as *communitas*). Without such exuberantly creative groups, the "creative chaos of liminality"[8] does not occur. Hungarian liminality produces only adversarial factioning, which in turn leads to greater social division and chaos. The lack of *communitas*, Hankiss says, means that Hungarian society's successful transcendence of its communist legacy and symbolic integration into the European and global community is at risk.

Hankiss's depiction of negative Hungarian liminality is supported by a number of scholarly and journalistic accounts of contemporary Hungarian social and political reality. For example, the coexistence of "multiple Hungarys" is a theme that continues to surface in Hungarian political science and sociology. What I refer to as the multiple Hungarys thesis suggests that social, economic, and political divisions in Hungary have such long historical roots and run so deep that the country is best thought of as a loose unity of two or three irreconcilable parts. In a classic essay, the political scientist Gyula Tellér envisions the tripartite division of the Hungary's "political force field" by three competing social traditions present in the country.[9] Conservatives are the descendants of Hungary's feudal past, liberals inherited the cosmopolitan impulse of the pre–World War II urban bourgeoisie, and socialists continue the tradition established by communism. These social groups possess different degrees of social, economic, and political influence, with socialists coming out on top by virtue of being directly affiliated with the communist political and economic elite. Another version of the multiple Hungarys thesis asks whether Hungarian society is marked by an irreparable split between a political left and right.[10] Writer and MP Endre Kukorelly had a blunt answer to this question: Hungarian society "had been sawed into two halves. It had been split with a battle-axe."[11]

Reflecting on the negative, or even destructive, nature of Hungarian public discourse, the Swiss *Neue Zürcher Zeitung* stated that, more than any other country in the region, Hungarian politics tended to turn any and all social or economic issues into party politics.[12] Hungarian parties sought out every opportunity to attack one another and avoid constructive negotiations and compromise at all costs. The main reason behind these "hate orgies by the Danube" (*Hassorgien an der Donau*) was that Hungary had been less successful in transferring economic and political power from communist elites to reformers than had countries like Slovakia or the Czech Republic. In Hungary, the *NZZ* argued, communists were still in control because they had been able to quickly transform themselves into a social democratic political platform and thus prevented a popular resistance movement. Tellér elaborates on this point: because the 1989 regime change did not provide an adequate release for revolutionary impulses (i.e., the ruling class was not directly challenged or swept away by a revolutionary class), these impulses found an outlet in social tensions which, in turn, fueled political tensions.[13]

Tamás expands this history of political tension to include the country's entire political history from the Hungarian Revolution of 1848 to the present day.[14] For the past century and a half, Hungarian politics has been a continuous "civil war" fought by political factions. "Hatred" in this context, he says, meant two things: a continued challenge to the legitimacy of those in power, and denying the need for political opposition. To be in political opposition in Hungary, Tamás explains, meant wishing for the extinction of the rulers, or at least their exclusion from the public sphere. To be in power, on the other hand, meant desire for complete control and ownership of the nation. Such control included ostracizing the opposition from the public sphere. This deeply antidemocratic historical and political legacy prevents today's Hungarian political system from forging the two Hungarys into one.

Liminality and "Hate Speech"

In its current form, "hate speech" as a concept and a term for communicative action made its public appearance in Hungary in 1996. In an interview with the social psychologist György Csepeli, the journalist asked Csepeli to clarify what he had meant when he characterized the propaganda of a pro-Nazi group as *gyűlöletbeszéd*.[15] Csepeli explained that talk was not mere information but action.[16] Derogatory talk about Jews injured the self-esteem and identity of members of the target group. Therefore, he suggested, such talk ought to be thought of as criminal action and speakers of hate speech should face criminal trials.

The journalist and Csepeli were not discussing hate speech in general, but rather a particularly controversial trial in the course of which the leader of the above-mentioned group, Albert Szabó, and his associates were acquitted of charges of incitement against a community by the Metropolitan Court of Budapest. Legal discourse has decisively shaped the use of the term "hate speech" in allegations of, and talk about, such actions. In the Hungarian context, allegations of hate speech often invoke legal definitions of the term, and public discussion about the issue frequently gravitates toward interpreting the legal implications of speaking hate speech in public. For example, hate speech is often discussed as the violation of human dignity.[17] According to Pál, Hungarian legal scholars interested in the limits of free expression began to use the term in the early 1990s.[18] Indeed, the constitutional scholar Gábor Halmai used an earlier version of the term, *gyűlölködő beszéd* (speech expressing hatred), in 1994.[19] With the appearance of *gyűlöletbeszéd*, "speech expressing hatred" did not vanish from public discourse, but most significant and consequential public debates unfolded around the meaning and use of the former.

Digging deeper into the history of the term, we find that a long legal history of regulating public discourse preceded the appearance of hate speech on the Hungarian cultural scene. Györgyi's discussion of the legal history of *gyűlöletbeszéd* locates the origin of legal responses to the concept in the first Hungarian criminal code, called the Csemegi Code.[20] The creation of the code was part of the legal reform in the wake of the 1867 Austro-Hungarian Compromise, a political deal that led to Hungary becoming a constitutional monarchy and an equal partner with Austria within the Habsburg Monarchy. Published in 1878 and named after its primary author, the Transylvanian lawyer György Csemegi, the Csemegi Code called for the criminal punishment of expression that qualified as incitement against the state and social order. Public expression challenging the legitimacy of the throne, royal succession, or the general assembly, and derogatory public expression directed at religion, race, and ethnicity were seen to fall outside the scope of free expression. This came as a response to social and political upheaval brought about by the Compromise during the last decades of the nineteenth century. Some would refer to this political age as yet another chapter in Hungary's troubled history; Hankiss would most likely describe it as the nation's entry into liminal existence.

Hungarian society existed in a state of liminality at the time of all subsequent modifications of those parts of the criminal code that placed restrictions on free expression. In 1921, just one year after Hungary lost two-thirds of its area in the Treaty of Trianon on June 4, 1920, the criminal code was modified to outlaw "incitement to destabilize the state" (*államfelforgatásra izgatás*), "defamation of the nation" (*nemzetrágalmazás*), and "slander against the nation" (*nemzetgyalázás*). The state was so concerned with the communist and far-right threat to public order that the new law expanded criminal sanctions to public *and* private expression. In 1941, sanctions against derogatory talk targeting members of ethnicities were added. These modifications reflected the 1938 and 1940 Vienna Awards, which partially revised the Treaty of Trianon and expanded Hungary's borders. Both Awards were annulled immediately after World War II, and in 1946 Law VII introduced a significant distinction between "instigation to rebellion" (*lázítás*) and "incitement" (*izgatás*). The former category included public expression directed against democratic order and the Constitution; the latter included a wide variety of public statements ranging from incitement to hatred against the state and its institutions, political, religious, ethnic, racial groups, and the expression of praise for war criminals and for other speakers who committed incitement. As the country was recovering from the devastation of World War II, the 1946 law interpreted incitement, the most immediate legal predecessor of hate speech, as an act of sedition.

With the rise of the communist police state, the legal concept of incitement was modified twice. In 1961, incitement was expanded to include the public expression of sentiments against the Hungarian nation, the Hungarian People's Republic, and its international partners (i.e., the Soviet states). "Public" was defined as an audience of two or more listeners. The 1961 law modifying the criminal code introduced a new concept, "insults directed at particular groups" (*közösség megsértése*), a form of criminal offense that threatened public peace. Section 269 of Law IV of 1978 further specified this latter category to include not only racial, religious, or ethnic groups but also political groups of "socialist convictions." The communists' legal interpretation of incitement was used to persecute anyone publicly expressing even vaguely antiestablishment views, including the perfectly harmless Budapest-based punk rock group CPg in 1983.

The 1989 regime change, a shift that Tellér characterizes as "the quiet collapse of a chronically underachieving system stripped of its external support," brought about another revision of the criminal code.[21] The modification (Law XXV) deleted the legal category of incitement against the state and renamed the complementary category of public expression disturbing public peace "incitement against communities" (*közösség elleni izgatás*). The new law returned to the nineteenth-century legal practice of punishing certain forms of public expression that take place in front of large audiences—that is, audiences comprising more than two listeners. It also distinguished two kinds of communicative practices, "instigation to hatred" (*gyűlöletre uszítás*) and "derogatory remarks" (*lealacsonyító megjegyzések*), targeting the Hungarian nation, ethnic, religious, racial groups, or any group within the Hungarian population. While this distinction sounded clear enough in legal principle, it was difficult to put into practice.

The year 1989 also marked the beginning of a long series of public debates about hate speech, more particularly about section 269 of the 1978 law. These debates are punctuated by landmark decisions of the Hungarian Constitutional Court directed at protecting freedom of expression from the excesses of criminal law.[22] In 1992, under the influence of liberal constitutional scholars with Western educations, the Court declared unconstitutional the criminal sanctioning of "derogatory remarks" directed at particular groups. In its decision, the court cited the clear and present danger test Judge Oliver Wendell Holmes used in a landmark U.S. Supreme Court decision.[23] In 1996, the Hungarian Parliament expressed outrage about the Metropolitan Court's decision to acquit Albert Szabó and his fellow extremists by calling for additional protection for minorities in the criminal law. The Constitutional Court once again decided to protect freedom of expression and declared the bill unconstitutional. Political forces concerned with rising nationalism, xenophobia, anti-Semitism, and anti-Roma discrimination continued to call for and sponsor bills designed to impose more severe criminal sanctions on incitement against communities. The Court evaluated subsequent bills in a manner similar to its 1992 decision in 1999 and 2004. Some politicians and legal experts intent on providing Hungarian citizens with additional safeguards against hate speech responded to this series of failures by advocating modifications to the civic instead of the criminal code. Other members of the Hungarian elite continue to argue the merits of criminalizing hate speech.

Although in the end the debate did not affect the original 1978 wording of section 269, it did generate three amendments. The amendments sanction publicly made derogatory remarks about national symbols (the national flag, the national anthem, and the country's coat of arms), the public display of communist and Nazi symbolism, and the public denial of Nazi and communist crimes against humanity.

This brief overview of the legal history of hate speech, and the emergence of "incitement against communities" as the legal equivalent of "hate speech" in particular, shows that public concern with the issue and the experience of liminality are inseparable in the Hungarian context. When the social order seems to fall apart, Hungarians seek to cleanse public expression.

A Social Drama: The Hegedűs Affair

Negative liminality is not simply a cultural critic's abstract diagnosis of Hungarian social relations. The so-called Hegedűs affair, which remains the most widely cited case of *gyűlöletbeszéd* to this day in Hungary, was a painful confrontation with such liminality. As does Hankiss, I, too, rely on the work of Victor Turner,[24] an anthropologist preoccupied with crisis and cultural norms, to show that Hungarians experienced the affair as a social drama, "a dramatic sequence in which social actors manifest concern with, and negotiate the legitimacy and scope of, the group's rules of living."[25]

Here, I present findings from the analysis of four excerpts from a corpus of 355 media texts (reports, articles, letters to the editor) published between 2001 and 2003, the time frame of the social drama that unfolded in the wake of the publication of a controversial article in a small district newsletter of a then-influential radical right-wing party. My goal is to introduce a theme that I will more fully develop in chapter 2, the diversity of Hungarian folk interpretations of hate speech. Although the Hegedűs affair did not bring into play the full range of meanings Hungarians assigned to *gyűlöletbeszéd*, the following discussion of the affair should give the reader a taste of the lack of consensus about the term's meaning.

The individual at the center of the controversy was the Hungarian Calvinist pastor Lóránt Hegedűs, Jr., the son of Calvinist bishop Lóránt Hegedűs. In August 2001, Hegedűs was also serving as the deputy chairman of the largest Hungarian party on the radical right, MIÉP (the Hungarian Justice and Life Party), and was a member of the Hungarian Parliament during the rule of the dominant conservative party Fidesz. On August 16, 2001, Hegedűs published an article titled "Christian Hungarian State!" in a district newsletter (*Ébresztő* [Wake-up call]) of a Budapest chapter of MIÉP. The time of the article's publication was not a coincidence. August 20 is a national holiday in Hungary marked by festivities celebrating Hungarian nationhood. The day is also dedicated to Stephen I, the first monarch of Hungary and a Christian saint, who transformed an alliance of Hungarian tribes into the sovereign Hungarian kingdom in 1000 CE. Today, not all Hungarians celebrate the Christian roots of the Hungarian nation and state on August 20; the title of the controversial article clearly aligned the author with those who did.

The argument Hegedűs puts forward in the article can be summed up as follows: Ill-willed and destructive Jews had decided to strip Hungary of its essential character as a Christian state. They are trying to accomplish this by accusing those who regard Hungary a Christian state of social exclusion. Hence, in order to protect the essential character of the Hungarian nation, Jews must be excluded. The excerpted parts below indicate which sentences were most widely discussed and evaluated in the Hungarian media as *gyűlöletbeszéd* following the article's publication.

The Compromise[26], or self-surrender, resulted in the arrival of the hordes of Galician vagrants[27] who, as the incarnations of people of yore,[28] chewed and continue to chew to pieces the nation that, even in its ruins, on the bones of the heroes, still, despite all circumstances, always, again and again, is capable of resurrection. Their Zion of the Old Testament was lost because of their sins and revolts against God, and so they say: let the Hungarian Zion, the most promising culmination[29] of the New Testament order of life, be destroyed.

Ady[30] also says of the Hungarian Zion: "So many desires, passions, and Jews have never raged in a people. . . . " And since not all Palestinians can be smoked out from beside the banks of the Jordan with fascistic methods that often put the Nazis to shame, they are coming again to the banks of the Danube, sometimes in the guise of internationalism, or in the guise of nationalism, or of cosmopolitanism, to give the Hungarian [nation] another kick, because they feel like it.

They are hysteric when they hear this form of address: CHRISTIAN HUNGARIAN STATE.

They claim: to say [that Hungary is a Christian state] constitutes exclusion.

So hear, Hungarian, in the one thousandth year of the Christian Hungarian state the only message that leads to life, the one based on a thousand years' ancient inheritance and continuity of law: EXCLUDE THEM! BECAUSE IF YOU DO NOT, THEY WILL DO IT TO YOU![31]

The publication of the article was met with public outcry on the political left and in some segments of the political right. The parts of the article that attracted the most criticism were the sentences widely regarded as instances of hate speech, especially the last part, where the author calls overtly for discrimination against Jews. The Prosecutor General's Investigation Office launched a criminal investigation against Hegedűs Jr. and György Metes, the publisher of *Ébresztő*, on September 19, on the charge of anti-group incitement. The next day, the Reformed Church of Hungary officially condemned the article and announced that the text was not in accordance with the teachings of Calvinism. On October 4, the scandal spilled over the borders of Hungary when the Swiss *Basler Zeitung* reported on the Hegedűs affair. At the request of the Prosecutor General the Hungarian

Parliament suspended Hegedűs's parliamentary immunity. He was subpoenaed and appeared in court for the first time on January 18, 2002. He was charged with incitement on June 15, 2002, and was found guilty by the Budapest Metropolitan Court on December 6. Hegedűs was ultimately acquitted in the Budapest Metropolitan Court of Appeals on November 6, 2003.[32]

From a cultural perspective, the question to be asked is, How did Hungarians make sense of this incident? Viewing the affair as a social drama helps us understand the local significance of this incident and its aftermath. Victor Turner's theory of social drama[33] and Philipsen's subsequent discussion of it[34] suggest that social dramas consist of four phases: (1) a breach of local, communal norms, (2) crisis leading to the formation of social factions, (3) attempts at redressing the crisis, and (4) communal reintegration, or open recognition of schism. The breach of sociocultural norms that occurred with the publication of the article was officially recognized when the Hungarian media reported that the General Prosecutor's Office launched a criminal investigation against Hegedűs and Metes. The discussion of hate speech that the breach prompted revealed the gaping ideological and moral rifts in the fractured Hungarian public. In Turner's analysis of social drama, "the narrative component in ritual and legal action attempts to rearticulate opposing values and goals in a meaningful structure, the plot of which makes cultural sense."[35] Accordingly, the crisis phase of the Hegedűs affair became a site for the public negotiation and construction of the meaning of hate speech in Hungary. In the end, Hegedűs's acquittal signaled that attempts to rearticulate Hungarian society as a whole had failed. This social drama ended with the image of Hegedűs's supporters carrying him out of the courtroom on their shoulders, and with embittered statements from representatives of the political left. Hankiss's discussion of negative liminality creating more opportunities for factioning than for creative, visionary problem solving, resonates with this conclusion.[36] If Hungarian society, according to Hankiss, is frozen in a state of liminality without *communitas*, it can also be said to exist in a perpetual state of crisis.

The Many Meanings of "Hate Speech"

The sociocultural crisis that engulfed Hungarian society for years after Hegedűs affair gives us a glimpse into the proliferation of meanings Hungarians assign to "hate speech." The Hungarian daily newspaper *Magyar Hírlap* was one of the first media outlets to respond to the publication of the Hegedűs article. In the report, the socialist politician Magda Kósáné Kovács characterizes the article as *gyűlöletbeszéd*. Her reaction to the Hegedűs article is relatively close to the U.S. American interpretation of the term.

Excerpt 1.1[37]

A gyűlöletbeszédnek ez a mélysége fasisztoid, és nem lehet büntetlenül hagyni—mondta lapunknak Kósáné Kovács Magda, az emberi jogi bizottság szocialista elnöke. A történelemből tudjuk, hogy az antiszemitizmus, a zsidók kirekesztése és megkülönböztetése vezetett a kristályéjszakához—véli a politikus. Kósáné Kovács Magda szerint a legfőbb ügyésznek fel kell vetni azt a kérdést, hogy a MIÉP működése még az alkotmányos kereteken belül van-e.

"Such a depth of hate speech shows fascistic tendencies, and it must not pass unpunished," Magda Kósáné Kovács, chairwoman of the parliamentary Committee on Human Rights, told [*Magyar Hírlap*]. "We know from history that anti-Semitism, the exclusion and discrimination of Jews, led up to Kristallnacht," the politician argued. According to Kósáné, the Chief Prosecutor must examine whether the operations of MIÉP are still within the limits of constitutionality.[38]

Kósáné discusses hate speech as the performance of a single speaker, directed at Hungarian Jews. The politician invokes Hegedűs's call for "exclusion" and links it to similar performances that had taken place during the days preceding World War II and the large-scale extermination of Jews. Kósáné sees a pattern: across the ages, hate speech had the potential to harm society. As a result, she argues for the sanctioning of both the speaker and the speaker's social group.

Besides identifying particular interpretations of *gyűlöletbeszéd* in media texts, it is equally interesting to identify missing symbolic elements that are commonly associated with *gyűlöletbeszéd*. Looking at further excerpts from media texts, it becomes apparent that at least two such features, the identification of addressees as members of historically disadvantaged minorities and the emotion of hatred in the speaker (expressed through the emotional style of delivery), are both treated as optional in Hungarian interpretations of hate speech in public discourse. For example, the excerpt below, from the written summary of a broadcast discussion of hate speech, locates emotions relevant to hate speech in the target and the audience but not the speaker.

Excerpt 1.2

A vendégek először a gyűlöletbeszéd fogalmát definiálták. Ha valaki rossz viszonyban van a feleségével, s gyűlölködve beszél róla, az még nem gyűlöletbeszéd. Ez társadalmi csoportokat sért, és bennük félelmet gerjeszt, mégpedig átgondoltan és tudatosan. Amikor a félelem gerjesztődik, akkor a sértegetésnek már egy olyan szintjére jut, hogy valószínűleg a társadalmi normák nevében föl kell ez ellen lépni.

Egy hallgató szerint a szocialistákra folyamatosan a gyűlöletbeszéd jellemző, példaként azt hozta fel, hogy 23 millió román vendégmunkással riogatták az embereket. A szakértő szerint azért kell óvatosan bánni a definíciókkal, mert a politikai viták tele vannak szenvedéllyel, a politikusok, különféle oldalon álló politikusok nagyon sokszor mondanak olyan dolgokat, amelyek később nem bizonyulnak igaznak. Megpróbálják érzelmileg is maguk mögé állítani a szavazókat.

Our guests [political scientist János Simon and sociologist András Kovács] began by defining hate speech. It is not hate speech if someone is in a bad relationship with his wife and speaks of her with hatred. Hate speech offends groups and arouses fear in them in a strategic and conscious manner. When fear is aroused, the offense reaches a level at which point it must be sanctioned on the basis of social norms.

According to a caller, the socialists are characterized by the constant use of hate speech. As an example, the caller brought up how the Socialists used the prospect of twenty-three million Romanian guest workers flooding the country [as a result of the conservative movement's labor policy] to frighten the public.[39] According to the expert, one must use definitions carefully because political debates are full of passion and politicians along the entire political spectrum often say things that later prove to be false. They attempt to win over voters emotionally.[40]

This excerpt suggests that the expression of hatred for someone does not qualify as hate speech. What does is when it is directed against groups of people, "and arouses fear in them in a strategic and conscious manner." Hate speech is framed as strategic communicative action that is carried out for the purpose of arousing fear in a group. "Frighten[ing]" the public, "political debates are full of passion," and "win[ning] over voters emotionally" again locate emotion in an actor or a group of actors other than the individual speaker. The enactment of hate speech therefore does not necessitate emotion in the speaker. What the excerpt seems to suggest is that the more calculated and strategic hate speech is, the more likely it is to trigger the desired emotional response.

Excerpt 1.3 below illustrates that there is no consensus about whom the likely targets of *gyűlöletbeszéd* may be. Columnist Dávid Megyeri argues that an entire government can be guilty of hate speech against dissenting thinkers.

Excerpt 1.3

Régóta terítéken tartja a kormánykoalíció a gyűlöletbeszéd elleni fellépés tematikáját, hogy egyfajta közös ellenséget fabrikálva kovácsolhassák egybe a korántsem koherens baloldali-liberális tábort. Annyi bizonyos azonban, hogy a legkevésbé sem igyekeznek a saját portájukon söpörni, azaz a másként gondolkodókkal szembeni gyűlölet keltésére irányuló megnyilatkozásaikat kordába szorítani. Holott akár el is fogadhatnák saját, MSZP-s frakcióvezetőjük definícióját az úgynevezett gyűlöletbeszéddel kapcsolatban. Lendvai Ildikó úgy fogalmazott: "Büntethető lenne az a bizonyos gyűlöletbeszéd, ami másokat komoly kárral fenyeget. Tehát, amely cselekvésre is buzdíthat adott esetben egy másik társadalmi csoport kirekesztése vagy jogfosztása érdekében." ... A szocialista–szabad demokrata kabinet nem csupán a független, demokratikus intézmények nem általuk kinevezett vezetőit támadja, hanem mindazokat, akik az övékétől eltérő nézeteket, illetve érdekeket akarnak képviselni.

The government coalition has been keeping the topic of anti–hate speech action in the forefront for awhile now in order to forge the leftist–liberal camp, which is currently far from coherent, into a unified whole. It is obvious that they make no attempt to clean up their own act and to control their own statements intended to incite hatred against those who think differently. They should consider adopting their own faction leader's definition of so-called hate speech. Ildikó Lendvai said, "The type of hate speech that threatens others with serious harm would become punishable. That is, the type [of hate speech] that might also encourage action designed to serve the exclusion or disenfranchisement of another social group." ... The Socialist–Free Democrat cabinet is attacking not only those leaders of independent, democratic institutions whom they did not appoint but everyone who stand for views or interests other than theirs.[41]

The left-wing government's charges of hate speech, Megyeri argues, serve the purpose of uniting the left against a common enemy, the political right. Such use of hate speech as an allegation meets the abstract criteria of *gyűlöletbeszéd*, which were formulated and advocated by the very same coalition. The left arouses hatred against the right in a calculated manner by labeling their institutions and dissenting views as hate speech.

We have seen that in some Hungarian public discourse the emotion of hatred in the speaker and the identity of the target are nonessential features of hate speech. The ethnographer, whose job it is to map the full range of cultural meanings, cannot simply follow the dominant sense-making strategy and privilege the interpretation of hate speech as the expression of hatred against nondominant social groups. In addition, the materials used here indicate that there are other elements of communication commonly associated with *gyűlöletbeszéd* whose relevance to enactments of the practice are uncertain or contested.

Type of speaker. Speakers accused of hate speech often speak from a political persona, but the location of this persona on the political spectrum varies. The identity of the social group in which the speaker claims membership may vary as well. The range of possible identities includes Lóránt Hegedűs, Jr., a conservative Christian politician (excerpt 1.1); left-wing politicians (excerpts 1.2 and 1.3); or whoever left-wing politicians think is guilty of hate speech (excerpt 1.3).

Relative social influence of speaker and target. Although both excerpts 1.1 and 1.3 indicate that Hegedűs or the socialist–liberal coalition attempt to exercise power over their addressees by speaking hate speech, the segments also propose that these attempts can be revealed and defused.

Variety of communicative act types interpreted as hate speech. Hate speech as a communicative act is variously associated with expressions of "anti-Semitism," "discrimination," and "exclusion" (excerpt 1.1), "offense" and "frightening the public" (excerpt 1.2), and "threaten[ing] others with serious harm" (excerpt 1.3).

The historical pattern associated with hate speech. Public discourse sometimes utilizes historical patterns to make sense of hate speech. At other times, hate speech is discussed in an abstract, atemporal sense. Excerpt 1.1 relates hate speech to the rise of fascism in pre–World War II Germany and suggests that Hegedűs's hate speech may be an indication that fascism is about to resurface on the Hungarian political scene. Excerpt 1.3, on the other hand, locates the practice of hate speech in recognizable patterns of contemporary Hungarian politicking.

Proposed sanctions. Excerpt 1.1 alludes to the potential criminal implications of Hegedűs's hate speech and the possibility of pronouncing Hegedűs' entire political party unconstitutional in the wake of the controversial article's publication. Excerpt 1.3, in contrast, proposes no such legal sanctions, but rather calls on the government coalition to exercise self-sanctioning.

In the light of these uncertainties, it seems that Hungarians have limited agreement about the meaning of hate speech. Still, based on the discussion so far, it also seems safe to claim that the Hungarian term "hate speech" does have a core meaning: it is a locally recognized form of public expression. That claim, however, misrepresents the full range of meanings of the term. Consider an excerpt from an op-ed piece written by the journalist Gyula Krajczár. In contrast to previous excerpts, the excerpt below calls into question whether hate speech in the Hungarian context denotes observable public talk at all.

Excerpt 1.4

Nekem fogalmam sincs arról, hogy amikor eredetileg kitalálták a gyűlöletbeszéd szót, az pontosan írta-e le azt, amire használták. Abban viszont biztos vagyok, hogy mai magyarországi népszerűsége egy gyökeresen új jelentéstartalomnak köszönhető. Valaki szövegének gyűlöletbeszéddé minősítése nem más, mint sajnálkozás afölött, hogy az illető egyáltalán szóra nyithatja a száját. Régebben ezt úgy mondták magyarul, hogy "Pofa be!" A félelemkeltés ismeretesebb szó, s lényegében ugyanerre a szituációra használják azok, akik már nem szeretnének újat tanulni. Erre a jelentésmódosulásra volt szükség ahhoz, hogy a kifejezések egyenletesen borítsák el a teljes politikai palettát. Ez a jelentés kellett ahhoz, hogy ma már Pokorni is azt mondhassa az ellenzék összes megnyilvánulását összefoglalandó, hogy gyűlöletbeszéd. Pofa be! Ez kellett ahhoz, hogy az árvízvédelmi kormányember azt mondhassa a munkáját kritizáló Szekeresnek, hogy félelemkeltés. Mégiscsak elegánsabban hangzik, mint amire valójában gondolt: pofa be!

I have no idea whether at the time they came up with the word hate speech it was a precise characterization of what it was used to characterize. Nonetheless, I am quite sure that its current Hungarian popularity is the result of an entirely different meaning. Evaluating someone's talk as hate speech is simply the expression of sorrow regarding the unfortunate fact that the other is entitled to open his or her mouth. Some time ago what they used to say in Hungarian was "Shut up!" The arousal of fear is a better-known term, and is essentially used in the same types of situations by people who don't wish to hear new things. This shift in meaning was necessary for the expression to evenly cover the entire political spectrum. This meaning was necessary for Pokorni to sum up everything the opposition does as hate speech. Shut up! It was necessary for the government official responsible for flood control to respond to Szekeres's criticisms by characterizing them as the arousal of fear. This is a much more elegant way of saying what he really thought: Shut up![42]

Krajczár indicates that he is not concerned with precise definitions of hate speech or with the creation of one. Definitions seem secondary in importance to the rhetorical function and power of "hate speech" (and a related term, "the arousal of fear") in political discourse. Here, hate speech is presented as an empty signifier, the sole function of which is to silence an opponent. Hate speech underwent a "shift in meaning" that enabled Hungarian politicians of all stripes to use it as a rhetorical weapon to silence criticism. As one of my interviewees put it, hate speech can be seen as a *kommunikációs balta vagy bunkó* (a communicative axe or club) one can wield with the hope of threatening and silencing one's political adversaries.

Hegedűs's acquittal marked Hungarian society's failure to achieve reintegration in the face of hate speech. The indeterminacy of the meaning of *gyűlöletbeszéd*, the term widely used in Hungary to name the issue, contributed in a large way to this failure. Not only do public speakers disagree about what types of talk constitute hate speech, some of them call into question whether hate speech should be interpreted at all as actual, observable talk. The next chapter catalogs the diverse meanings of *gyűlöletbeszéd*.

2

DIVERSITY OF MEANING

"Hate speech" is not only a social issue; it is also a term for a type of communicative action. The meanings of the term, as we will see, affect the meaning of the issue. Participants in public debates about hate speech or any other social issue that they refer to with a hotly contested term (such as "terrorism" or "poverty") must learn to navigate a terrain of meanings associated with that term in order to be seen as competent participants. In the case of hate speech, a competent participant has a sense of the type (or types) of communicative action the term stands for. Mapping the various meanings of a term used to name an issue is an essential task in the quest to understand the social life of that issue.

The act of mapping meanings requires cartographic methodology. Let us momentarily shelve the observation that there is a small number of Hungarians who call into question the claim that hate speech points to actual, observable acts of speaking in public—I will return to this interpretation in chapter 5. Here, I pursue the interpretation of *gyűlöletbeszéd* as a type of observable talk, and rely on the theory and methodology of cultural terms for communicative action research,[1] a branch of cultural discourse analysis.[2] From this perspective, *gyűlöletbeszéd* is a term that acquires meaning in discourse, the patterned, context-bound use of language.[3]

The cultural meanings of a cultural term for communicative action fall into three categories. Cultural communities of speakers interpret such terms as *acts* performed by individual speakers, as *events* (or co-enactments involving multiple participants, including the speaker), and as *style* (a selection from among a number of available choices). The three levels of interpretation may, potentially, inform the analyst of fundamental cultural beliefs about what persons are, how they relate to one another in society, and how they communicate. I use data from seventeen broadcast discussions of hate speech and from the collection of media texts discussing the Hegedűs affair to show just how complex the meaning of the term is in contemporary Hungarian public discourse, and what that complexity tells us about Hungarian beliefs about communicating in public.

Act-Level Interpretations

Speakers make sense of hate speech and other terms for communicative action at the act level as individual performances of communication. In a survey of seventeen episodes of broadcast talk about hate speech, I was able to identify forty-four other terms for communicative action speakers used to interpret hate speech as an act of speaking by an individual speaker. Table 2.1 presents these interpretations in the order they appear for the first time in my data. This long and amorphous list of folk labels for speech points to folk models of hate speech as communicative action. It appears that act-level interpretations fall into five categories depending on what particular element of the communicative act the interpretation highlights: the speaker, the message, the target, the audience, or the communicative event.

Speaker-oriented interpretations describe hate speech as stemming from an attitude or disposition in the speaker. This category includes such interpretations of hate speech as "racist talk," "expression of anti-Gypsyism," "expression of misogyny," "expression of xenophobia," "expression of anti-Semitism," "expression of disdain toward the marginalized poor," and "speech expressing hatred." These terms for talk present the act of speaking as evidence of prejudice in the speaker. The talk expresses the type of person, and the person expresses the talk: a racist person speaks in a racist way because he or she is racist, and the person is racist because he or she speaks in a racist way. Also, implicitly or explicitly, speaker-oriented interpretations associate the speaker of hate speech with a group that is somehow presented as different from, and opposed to, the target group. For example, "racist talk" pits a speaker against a racial group to which he or she does not belong; a speaker who uses the "expression of misogyny" tends not to be a woman; an "expression of xenophobia" involves a speaker who positions him- or herself as the citizen of a country as opposed to noncitizens. An example of this type of interpretive orientation is typical in sociological investigations of hate speech, as illustrated in the following excerpt from a radio broadcast. The speaker, a Hungarian sociologist, argues that the majority of respondents in a survey designed to measure the public's anti-Semitic attitudes reject anti-Semitic public expression, which he takes as public support for legislation regulating hate speech.

Excerpt 2.1

Csináltam egy olyan közvéleménykutatást egy pár éve amely arra kérdezett rá, hogy ez az antiszemita előítéletekkel volt kapcsolatos, és amely arra

Table 2.1   Act-level interpretations of "hate speech"

Hungarian term	English translation
rasszista beszéd	racist talk
holokauszt-tagadás	Holocaust denial
emberek megalázása, méltóságának megsértése (csoporthoz tartozás alapján)	humiliating people, offending their dignity (on the basis of their group membership)
a gyűlöletbeszéd konkrét példái	specific examples of "hate speech"
közösség elleni izgatás	incitement against a community
gyűlöletre uszítás, gyűlöletkeltés	incitement, instigation to hatred
cigányellenesség (kifejezése)	expression of anti-Gypsyism
nőgyűlölet (kifejezése)	expression of misogyny
idegengyűlölet (kifejezése)	expression of xenophobia
antiszemitizmus (kifejezése)	expression of anti-Semitism
kitaszított szegények lenézése (lenézésének kifejezése)	expression of disdain toward the marginalized poor
kirekesztés, diszkrimináció	discrimination
megbélyegzés	stigmatization
kisebbségek, etnikumok ellen irányuló beszéd	negative talk about minorities, ethnicities
erőszakra és/vagy kiirtásra uszítás	incitement to violence and/or extermination
felháborító, undorító eszmék képviselése	representing abhorrent, disgusting views
téves, helytelen eszmék képviselete	representing mistaken, misguided views
gyűlölettel teli beszéd	speech filled with hatred
előítéletesség, előítéletek kifejezése	expression of prejudiced attitudes, prejudices
gyűlölködő beszéd	speech expressing hatred
gyűlölet (kifejezése)	(expression of) hatred
csoportok megsértése, fenyegetése	offending, threatening minorities
vallásában megsérteni valakit	to offend someone's religion
homofóbia (kifejezése)	expression of homophobia
fasizmus, nácizmus (kifejezése)	expression of fascism, Nazism
szóbeli erőszak	verbal violence
egy nemzet elleni gyűlöletre izgatás	incitement to hatred against a nation
negatív kijelentés csoport ellen	a negative remark about a group
leértékelő kijelentés csoport ellen	a derogatory remark about a group
félelem gerjesztése egy csoportban	arousing fear in a group

continued

Table 2.1   Act-level interpretations of "hate speech" (*continued*)

Hungarian term	English translation
hazugság (politikai stratégia elemeként)	telling lies (as an element of political strategy)
politikai csoportot gyűlöletbeszéddel vádolni	charging a political group with hate speech
vélemények kimondása tények helyett	expressing opinions instead of facts
érték- és/vagy normarendszer megsértése	offending one's system of values and/or norms
negatív politikai kampány	negative political campaigning
fasiszta, náci szimbólumok használata	the use of fascist, Nazi symbols
durva politikai vita	offensive political debate
magyarokról felháborító dolgokat mondani	to say outrageous things about Hungarians
egy csoport jogainak megsértése	violating a group's rights
olyan beszéd, amely kizárja a racionális választ	talk that precludes a rational response
az érzelmekre hatni akaró beszéd	talk designed to stir up emotions (in an audience)
csoport tagjainak fizikai megsemmisítésére felszólítás	calling for the physical extermination of members of a group
agresszív beszéd	aggressive talk
gyűlöletbeszéddel való vád	charging someone with hate speech

kérdezett rá, így szólt a kérdés, hogy ön szerint terjeszthessék-e szabadon nézeteiket azok, akik rendszeresen zsidóellenes kijelentéseket tesznek, s a válaszadók nyolcvannégy százaléka azt mondta hogy nem. Ne terjeszthessék. Tehát ez azt mutatja hogy van valamiféle társadalmi koszenzus is amögött hogy egy jól kialakított gyűlöletbeszéd-ellenes törvény létrejöhessen.

I conducted a public opinion survey a couple of years ago, asking respondents . . . the survey focused on anti-Semitic prejudice and we asked, the question was the following: Do you think those who make anti-Jewish statements on a regular basis should be allowed to disseminate their views freely? And 84 percent of respondents said no. They shouldn't. So this indicates that there is some sort of social consensus supporting the creation of well-drafted anti–hate speech legislation.[4]

Here, "anti-Jewish statements" are taken not only as manifest "anti-Semitic prejudice," they also qualify as "hate speech" to be regulated by law. This interpretation
of hate speech is interested in the speaker's act of public expression and locates
the source of that speech in the speaker's prejudiced attitudes toward groups
other than his or her own.

Message-oriented interpretations display concern with the content of the act
that constitutes hate speech. Interpretations that belong to this category are "Holocaust denial," "representing abhorrent, disgusting views" about ethnic minorities,
"representing mistaken, misguided views" of ethnic and racial groups, "the use of
fascist, Nazi symbols," and so on. The key element of hate speech, these interpretations suggest, is message content. Regardless of the identity of speaker, target,
or audience, displaying a Nazi swastika or voicing objectionable views about ethnic and racial target groups are instances of hate speech. In the next excerpt, the
speaker, a Hungarian free speech scholar, directs attention to the content of hate
speech as content laden with the tragic historical heritage of Europe.

Excerpt 2.2

A gyűlöletbeszéd szabályozásának ha lehet így mondani magyar modellje
azért is nagyon érdekes Európában és azt lehet mondani hogy világszerte
mert a gyűlölködő beszédnek és elsősorban a rasszista beszédnek a szig-
orúbb tartalmi alapon korlátozó szabályozása az elég jellemző Európára
és az emelletti egyik nagyon fontos érv az pontosan a borzalmas európai
történelem és annak az egyik nagyon borzalmas huszadik századi fejezete
a holokauszt.

Another reason why the Hungarian model of hate speech regulation is
very interesting in Europe and worldwide, we might say, is that the severe
content-based restriction of hateful speech and, specifically, racist speech
is fairly typical in Europe and one very important argument for [imposing
such restrictions] has been precisely the horrible history of Europe and
one particularly horrible twentieth-century chapter of that history, the
Holocaust.[5]

The European legislative framework, according to the speaker, identifies hate
speech on the basis of content. In this interpretation, "racist" and "hateful" talk
therefore qualifies as "hate speech" not because it reveals prejudice in the speaker
but because it carries certain types of content. Such content functions as the
breach of societal norms because it conjures up the Holocaust, the epitome of

racist genocide. Content-based orientations often treat hate speech as the manifestation of the history of hatred in the present.

Target-oriented interpretations—like "humiliating people, offending their dignity (on the basis of their group membership)," "offending, threatening minorities," "calling for the physical extermination of members of a group," or "talk that precludes a rational response"—foreground the (anticipated) effect of hate speech on a target or a group of targets. In this act-level interpretation, the target's reaction renders hate speech meaningful. Hate speech threatens, offends, or silences the target. An illustration of this interpretive orientation comes from the radio talk show *Szóljon hozzá!* (Have your say!). Explaining his position on the issue, a caller says that, to him, public talk can be interpreted as *gyűlöletbeszéd* only "if it serves the physical extermination [of] and the arousal of fear [in a group]" (ha már így kifejezetten fizikai megsemmisítésre és félelemkeltésre szolgál).[6]

A common thread that runs through these three interpretations is the depiction of hate speech as a mode of address designed to strip the target of the opportunity or ability to respond to the speaker as an equal. Hate speech is talked about as a communicative act designed to introduce, immediately and irrevocably, an asymmetrical relationship of status and power between speaker and target. The target (or group of targets) cannot respond as an equal because they have just suffered a violation either of their emotional stability (through humiliation or threats), of their group rights, or of their values, or because the speaker has violated the rules of rational debate and therefore prevented the target from producing a rational response.

A fourth, *audience-oriented* interpretation highlights the intended rhetorical effect of hate speech on a third-party audience. "Incitement to violence and/or extermination," "incitement to hatred against a nation," and "talk designed to stir up emotions (in an audience)" portray hate speech as an act of persuasion, as an attempt to motivate an audience to violent action by means of attitude change or emotionally charged rhetoric. We can see this interpretation active in the following excerpt from the above-mentioned episode of *Szóljon hozzá!*

Excerpt 2.3

Ugye a mai szabályozás ami érvényben van Magyarországon hiszen van korlátozás ez azt mondja ki, hogy a gyűlöletbeszéd az olyan, azok olyan kijelentések amelyek a megcélzott csoporttal szemben egy egyértelmű és világosan megjelenő veszélyt idéznek elő. De hát ez egy angolból átvett kategória a clear and present danger ez a kategóriája a ennek a következménynyel kell járnia a gyűlöletbeszédnek. Na most mik hogy lehet ezt leírni?

Hát ezek ilyen dolgokkal lehetne leírni hogy. A gyűlöletbeszéd például olyan ami erőszakot készít elő. Érdemileg előkészíti érzelmileg előkészíti az erőszakot. Egy olyasfajta beszéd ami kizárja a racionális érvelés lehetőségét az ellenérvek felsorolásának lehetőségét. Amelynek a célja tisztán az emóciók felkorbácsolása.

Well, according to regulations currently in effect in Hungary, because there are indeed regulations, regulations say that hate speech is a kind of utterance that places a target group into unequivocal and clearly present danger. Note that this is a category that had been adapted from English, the category of clear and present danger [English in the original] and this must be the consequence of hate speech. Now, how can we characterize hate speech? Well, here are some characteristics. Hate speech is for example [a kind of speech] that makes preparations for violence. It provides a substantial and emotional preparation. It is a kind of speech that precludes the opportunity for rational argumentation, the opportunity for counterarguments. Speech whose only objective is to whip up emotions.[7]

The speaker invokes the U.S. "clear and present danger" legal doctrine and casts hate speech as public expression that places a target group in harm's way. The *direct* source of the harm is, however, neither hate speech nor the person speaking hate speech. Harm, in this view, is visited upon the target group by an audience under the influence of hate speech. By whip[ping] up emotion, hate speech "provides a substantial and emotional preparation" for violence. In this interpretation, public expression is understood as a powerful rhetorical device that not only inspires a strong emotional response but also has the potential to "preclude the opportunity for rational argumentation, the opportunity for counterarguments." A captive audience willing to respond to the rhetoric of hate speech with violence against a group is a necessary element of this interpretation.

Finally, a fifth interpretation, "specific examples of 'hate speech,'" constitutes a category of its own as the only *event-oriented* interpretation of hate speech. Here, the meaning is bound to the event of its occurrence. The cultural logic of making sense of particular acts of hate speech is discussed in chapters 3 and 4.

The well-known Hungarian cartoonist Marabu's depiction of hate speech (fig. 2.1) captures the act-level interpretation well. We are presented with a lone speaker angrily firing speech bullets at a target. Although the target is vaguely shaped like a human, it is a cutout, a passive, nonhuman object that cannot respond to the towering hate speaker, and it bears only the mark of hateful words

Figure 2.1 Céltábla (Target), 2003. Political cartoon. Used by permission of Marabu

left on its surface. The destructive power of speech is met only by the target's passive vulnerability.

"Hate" plus "Speech"

Looking at act-level interpretations of hate speech, one may wonder what the semantic relationship is between *gyűlölet* (hate) and *beszéd* (speech) in *gyűlöletbeszéd*. As a casual experiment, I once asked a professional Hungarian–Arabic interpreter-translator how she would translate the term *gyűlöletbeszéd* into Arabic. She responded that a mirror translation of the term would not be meaningful to an Arabic speaker. Explicating the term in Arabic, she added, would pose problems of its own because it is difficult to tell what exactly "hate" had to do with "speech" in "hate speech." She suggested three interpretations of this relationship, all of which struck her as equally plausible: *gyűlöletből fakadó beszéd* (speech resulting from hatred), *gyűlöletet tartalmazó beszéd* (speech containing hatred), and *gyűlöletet keltő beszéd* (speech arousing hatred).

Table 2.1 provides us with clues about how Hungarian speakers try to reduce the semantic ambiguity resulting from the relationship between "hate" and "speech." Consider *gyűlölettel teli beszéd* (speech filled with hatred), *gyűlölködő beszéd* (speech expressing hatred), and *gyűlölet (kifejezése)* ([expression of] hatred). The first explication of the relationship between "hate" and "speech," "speech filled with hatred," conjures up an image of speech as a container for the speaker's emotions. The second explication (speech expressing hatred) presents speech as the locus and expressive medium of the speaker's hatred. The third ([expression of] hatred) locates hatred in the speaker and presents speech as a channel through which this hatred issues forth toward a target. The locus of hatred shifts in these folk terms from the speech, to the speaker, to its transmission from speaker to target. Each is related to the others, but each is not the same as the others.

The low degree of conventionalization has two important implications for Hungarian speakers discussing the meaning of hate speech in public. First, unless they happened to opt for the same interpretation of the relationship between "hate" and "speech," they need to spend some time and effort coordinating their interpretations of that relationship. Simply put, they need to do some work to make sure that they are indeed talking about the same thing. In Hungarian public discourse about hate speech, such an effort is rarely made. Speakers are eager to harness the term's moral force and use their own interpretation of hate speech to negatively evaluate others' speech. The second implication is that act-level interpretations have an important practical function: they provide templates for resolving the ambiguity of the relationship between "hate" and "speech."

Event-Level Interpretation

How is *gyűlöletbeszéd* talked about as a co-enactment by multiple parties, with particular types of outcomes? An infamous case of hate speech can give us some clues. The widely publicized controversy started on December 24, 2003, when a punk rocker (known throughout the Hungarian underground music scene as Barangó) made a controversial remark in a broadcast program of the Budapest community radio station Tilos Rádió (Forbidden radio). Barangó, who had had a drink or two before the show, and his cohosts were discussing depictions of Christian asceticism in Franco Zeffirelli's 1972 film *Brother Sun, Sister Moon*. At one point of the discussion, Barangó said that he refused to accept a religion that did not respect his physical instincts. When a cohost responded that no one forced him to accept Christianity and that he could just accept the existence of this religion without hating it, Barangó snapped, "No, I fucking can't! I would kill off all Christians! Wow, that's harsh" (Tud a faszom, bazdmeg! Kiirtanám az összes keresztényt! Huuuu, ez kemény).[8] Although Barangó's cohosts immediately distanced themselves from his remark, and Tilos Rádió promptly canceled the program and removed Barangó from the roster the following day, a major public controversy erupted.

In addition to the divisive nature of the remark, the subsequent controversy was fuelled by two other, related, remarks made earlier on Tilos Rádió. On December 9, 2003, one of the hosts suggested that the large wooden crosses installed by the conservative political movement Jobbik in various public areas throughout the country[9] should have been distributed to the poor as firewood. That decision, the host argued, would have been a much "more Christian act" (*keresztényibb cselekedet*).[10] A few days later, on December 19, on another program a host said, "No matter how we look at it or explain it, Christ was a bastard child" (Akárhogy is vesszük, magyarázzuk, Krisztus egy fattyú).[11]

In 2007, radio host Don Imus rocked the United States when he casually referred to African American players on the Rutgers women's basketball team as "nappy-headed hos" on the air. Barangó turned Hungary upside down. The day after the broadcast, a number of conservative political organizations (including the largest conservative political party, Fidesz) issued public condemnations of the program.[12] Police began investigating the incident on the suspicion of "incitement against a community."[13] The National Radio and Television Commission ruled that the radio station had to go off the air for a thirty-day period, and that the station would be excluded from the following round of applications for state funding. The regulatory body also issued an official second-strike warning to the station.[14] Gábor Csabai (better known among fans of the station as Papó), who served as the chairman of the station's advisory board at the time, told me in an interview on May 10, 2007, that the penalties meted out by the commission were some of the harshest received by any media organization in recent Hungarian broadcasting history.

Within weeks of Barangó's comments, two political demonstrations took place in front of Tilos Rádió's headquarters. Only about forty or fifty people attended the first, smaller-scale demonstration on January 6.[15] Five days later, thousands of people flooded Kinizsi Street in downtown Budapest carrying homemade banners bearing slogans like "Haters of Hungarians, abusers of Christians, get out" (Magyargyűlölők, kereszténygyalázók takarodjatok), "Act against hatred" (Tégy a gyűlölet ellen),[16] and "If you all hate Christians, go live among Muslims!!!" (Ha a keresztényeket gyűlölitek, éljetek a muzulmánok között!!!).[17] Orators made fiery speeches in which they castigated Tilos Rádió for harboring anti-Christian sentiments. One of the speakers, the poet Kornél Döbrentei, said, "There is [a law] the parliament shamefully passed, which protects them, the actual practitioners of hate speech. Well, they are doing their job all right" (Van viszont egy, szégyenszemre megszavazta a parlament, amely őket, a gyűlöletbeszéd valódi gyakorlóit oltalmazza. S lám, teszik is a dolgukat).[18] As the organized demonstration ended and the crowd began to disperse, two demonstrators burned an Israeli flag that a third demonstrator supplied. The organizers of the demonstration and conservative political organizations immediately condemned the act, and the police once again launched an investigation of incitement against a community. The three perpetrators were tried for breach of peace and later released on one to three years of probation.[19]

It may not be immediately clear to the outside observer how the burning of the Israeli flag can be seen as a sign of protest against the inebriated host of a radio program who expresses a desire to exterminate Christians. Papó, then chair of Tilos Rádió's advisory board, supplies the link. In an interview on May 10, 2007, he explained to me that the political right had long viewed Tilos Rádió as the voice of the liberal left. In addition, Tilos Rádió was equated with not only the liberal left but communists and Jews as well. In Hungary, Jews and communists have been portrayed as essentially interchangeable groups in radical conservative political discourse since the early part of the twentieth century.[20] Papó maintained that Barangó's misguided utterance was construed as hate speech because the Hungarian radical right got tired of being portrayed as nationalistic, fascistic, and anti-Semitic by the political left and was looking for an opportunity to "strike back." The utterance "I would kill off all Christians" was heard as an opportunity to show that the left can be just as guilty of hate speech as the right. My respondent put it as follows:

Excerpt 2.4

Ha tetszik ha nem, a liberális oldalról legalábbis a liberális gondolatkörből, egy olyan dolog hangzott el, aminek nem volt előzménye ilyen még nem volt, sőt és a liberális oldalról. A kommunisták oldaláról. A zsidók oldaláról ha úgy tetszik ilyen nem volt. És a jobboldal igyekezett minél több bőrt lehúzni erről.

Like it or not, something was spoken in the liberal political camp, or at least in the circles of liberal thought, that had no precedent, that had not happened before, and it came from the liberal camp, from the communist camp, from the Jewish camp, if you will. No such thing had come from there before. And the right tried to milk it as much as possible.

Burning the Israeli flag, therefore, constitutes a radical form of protest against what is seen as an unholy alliance of liberals, Jews, and Communists. The meaning of this symbolic act was at least partially echoed by one of the speakers at the demonstration in front of Tilos Rádió's studios on January 11, 2004. After exchanging jokes with audience members about the presence of secret agents planted in the audience by the left-wing government, the poet Kornél Döbrentei opened his speech with the following words:

Excerpt 2.5

Voltaképpen béketüntetésre gyűltünk itt össze, jó akaratú emberek. Mert az a jó, ha végre van akaratunk és késztetésünk tiltakozni a népünk megsemmisítésére törekvő, vallási köntösben folytatott engesztelhetetlen háború ellen. A magyarság erkölcsi holokausztja ellen, amelyet álpróféták, álruhában, álorcában, csak a szakálluk a valódi, vezényelnek.

Essentially we, people of good intentions, have gathered here for a peace demonstration. Because it is commendable if we, at last, have the will and the ambition to protest the unrelenting war, fought in the garb of religion, whose objective is the obliteration of our people. We protest the moral Holocaust of Hungarians, orchestrated by false prophets, wearing false clothes and masks—only their beards are real.

Although the speaker made no explicit derogatory remarks about Jews, the reference to the "false prophets, wearing false clothes and masks" whose "beards are real" was later interpreted as anti-Semitic insinuations by a number of leading Hungarian intellectuals, including the historian András Gerő.[21] Gerő argued that it was remarks like these that had prompted the burning of the Israeli flag after the demonstration.

My task, for now, is not to decide whether any of the utterances made in the context of this controversy constituted actual "hate speech"—my task is to trace communal interpretations of the term as accurately as possible. For example, one interesting aspect of this controversy from the perspective of cultural analysis is that both sides performed acts that prompted the police to launch investigations of incitement against a community. The police's reaction indicates that there had to be cultural perspectives from which calling both Barangó's talk about killing off Christians and the burning of the Israeli flag "hate speech" seemed sensible.

Let us return to the focal concern of this section, event-level interpretations of *gyűlöletbeszéd*. The analysis of the Tilos Rádió incident and the broadcast data indicates that all mentions of "hate speech" point to a core event-level interpretation. This interpretation suggests that hate speech is a co-enactment with a range of outcomes. First, as co-enactment, hate speech involves a speaker who deploys a message with reference to one or more of a target group's distinguishing features. The message offends or threatens that group or its members. The act of deploying the message positions the speaker as a member of a group different from the target group. A public audience acts as witness to the speaker's act, and a third-party judge of the act[22] evaluates the speaker's act as hate speech. Second, hate speech has four possible outcomes: some type of offense or sense of threat in the target; some type of negative response (e.g., outrage, disgust) in the third-party judge; the application of the term "hate speech" to the speaker's act by third-party judge; or the negative evaluation of the speaker's public persona.

The model of hate speech as a co-enactment constructs a coherent whole from the five act-level interpretations (speaker-, message-, target-, audience-, and event-oriented). Note, however, that the event-level model contains a new component, the third-party judge. At the event level of interpretation, hate speech implies an act of judgment (an allegation) that is never performed by speakers of hate speech.[23] Consider the opening of a call taken from a phone-in radio program, where the caller immediately positions herself as the third-party judge.

Excerpt 2.6

> HOST: Telefonszámunk háromszázhuszonnyolc hetvennyolc negyvenöt, újabb halgatónk van, halló halló? Halló? Halló halló?
> CALLER: Halló?
> HOST: Tessék parancsolni adásban van.

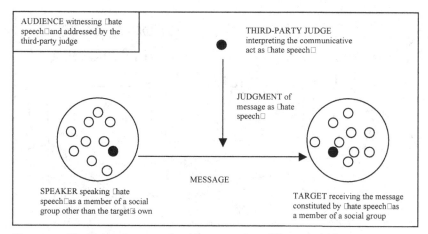

Figure 2.2   The Hungarian event-level interpretation of "hate speech"

CALLER: Jó napot kívánok, Radnóti Istvánné vagyok, három dolgot szeretnék mondani. Aztán lehet hogy több lesz belőle. Az egyik az hogy ha úgy vesszük két gyűlöletbeszéd már el is hangzott a hallgatók részéről.

HOST: Our telephone number is three twenty-eight seventy-eight forty-five. We have a new caller, hello hello? Hello? Hello hello?
Caller: Hello?
Host: Go ahead please, you are on the air.
CALLER: Good afternoon, I am Radnóti Istvánné. I would like to say three things. And then there may be more. One of them is that, in some way two hate speeches have already been spoken by listeners.[24]

The caller positions herself as third-person judge. In effect, this introductory self-positioning distances her from the "hate speeches"[25] of other "listeners" who had called into the program. Hate speech, from the Hungarian cultural perspective, cannot exist without such a judge. Figure 2.2 summarizes the event-level interpretation of hate speech. The role of the third-party judge in this interpretation is of key importance, and not only because without his or her assessment of someone else's talk there cannot be "hate speech." As we will see in subsequent chapters, the ethos of that judge, their credibility and their moral standing, is a central theme in Hungarian hate speech debates.

We can use this folk model of hate speech to make sense of another Marabu cartoon. This one (fig. 2.3) depicts the yard of a kindergarten with two young girls in a sandbox in the middle and two boys of the same age group standing nearby. One of the girls, her face contorted with anger, is yelling at the boys, "Boys! Boys!

Figure 2.3   Lila óvoda (Lila kindergarten), 2003. Political cartoon. Used by permission of Marabu

Their underwear has holes!" Outside the sandbox, the boys are jeering back, "Girls! Girls! Witches of the earth!" The caption reads, "As a result of the abuse of freedom of expression, hate speech rears its ugly head among middle group[26] children in the Lila kindergarten." The cartoon achieves its humorous effect by using the caption as the (somewhat self-righteous and sensationalistic) voice of the third-party judge who alleges hate speech where there is only harmless inter-gender mockery.

Style-Level Interpretations

Just as cartographers mapping a particular geographic area always attend to both the boundaries of that area and what lies on the other side of those boundaries, the cultural analyst mapping the meanings of a culture's key term must listen to and describe what lies beyond local interpretations of that term. Style-level interpretations tell us about the communal understanding of what type of speaking "hate speech" is *not*. Such contrast enriches the meaning of the term itself.

In broadcast talk, speakers contrast hate speech with other more or less established forms of talk, such as "love speech" (*szeretetbeszéd*), "political talk designed to arouse emotions" (*emóciókra apelláló politikai beszéd*), "rude talk" (*goromba beszéd*), "shocking views and political expression" (*meghökkentő nézetek és politikai megnyilvánulások*), or "democratic dialogue" (*demokratikus párbeszéd*). One type of contrast, however, seems more robust than do the others. In this interpretation, hate speech as an illegal and immoral form of expression is contrasted with other, perhaps controversial but nevertheless legal and morally acceptable forms that fall under the umbrella category of "free speech" or "free expression."

This interpretation, of course, tends to be endorsed by speakers who argue that "hate speech" ought to be illegal because it is immoral. This interpretation implies a causal relationship between the legality and morality of hate speech: *because* it is immoral it *ought to be* illegal. In the excerpt below, the socialist MP Gergely Bárándy, a staunch advocate of anti–hate speech legislation, draws on this interpretation. The host is asking Bárándy for his reaction to a statement by the liberal politician Gábor Fodor, who argued that the socialist proposal to outlaw hate speech was fundamentally misguided.

Excerpt 2.7

HOST: Azt mondta egyébként még ebben az interjúban hogy hogy ha valakit börtönbe zárnak majd különböző nézetek miatt akkor azokból majd mártírt csinálnak. Ha olyan eszméket fognak börtönbe zárni. Amilyenekről itt szó van akkor azok az eszmék tovább fognak terjedni, szóval hogy pont az ellenkező hatást érik ezzel, vélte ebben az interjúban Fodor Gábor.

BÁRÁNDY: Hadd emeljem azt ki hogy itt nem a meghökkentő nézetek. És a politikai megnyilánulásokat próbálják majd kordába szorítani ezzel a szabályozással vagy legalábbis őszintén remélem hogy—

HOST: De ő ettől tart.

BÁRÁNDY: De én őszintén remélem hogy nem így lesz. Én azt mondom, hogy kizárólag azokat a megnyilvánulásokat, amelyek súlyosan sértenek egyes népcsoportokat vagy társadalmi csoportokat. Ugyanúgy hadd hangsúlyozom hogy a szólásszabadságnak bizony vannak büntetőjogi korlátai, a mostani bétékában is, gondoljunk itt a rágalmazásra és a becsületsértésre.

Tehát nem igaz az hogy a szólásszabadság most ha úgy tetszik bétéká által nem szabályozott vagy nem korlátozott.

HOST: [Gábor Fodor] said in this interview that if someone went to prison for their various views they will be proclaimed martyrs. If you are going to imprison ideas that we are talking about here, those ideas will only spread further. I mean, you will achieve the exact opposite result, Gábor Fodor opined in this interview.

BÁRÁNDY: Let me emphasize that it is not shocking views and political expression that this law would be used to restrict, or at least I sincerely hope that—

HOST: But this is his concern.

BÁRÁNDY: But I sincerely hope that it will not be so. I said only those types of expression [should be restricted] that seriously offend certain national or social groups. Let me emphasize also that freedom of expression does have limits set by criminal law, in the present-day criminal code, consider libel and defamation. Therefore it is not true that freedom of expression today is not regulated or restricted, if you will, by the criminal code.[27]

What we see here is the negotiation of act- and style-level interpretations. Whereas the host (speaking for Fodor) interprets hate speech as "various views" and "ideas," Bárándy suggests a contrast between "shocking views and political expression" and "those types of expression that seriously offend certain national or social groups." "Shocking views and political expression" fall within the realm of "free expression." Hence, they cannot be subject to legal prohibitions and should not be seen as hate speech. Expression that offends groups, by contrast, is prohibited (i.e., not "free expression"), or at least should be, according to the speaker. Bárándy here works against an act-level interpretation that he hears implied in the host's presentation of Fodor's views. He attempts to accomplish this by introducing two contrasting act-level interpretations of hate speech ("shocking views and political expression" and "those types of expression that seriously offend certain national or social groups"), and then uses the first of the two as a style-level interpretation to argue what kind of speech does not qualify as hate speech because it is free expression. The caption of Marabu's second cartoon (fig. 2.3) also draws on this legalistic, style-level contrast between "hate speech" and "free speech" to achieve humorous incongruity between childhood digs at the opposite gender and derogatory talk targeting historically disadvantaged groups.

Messages About Communication

Having delved into the fine details of the meanings of Hungarian hate speech, it is time to create a comprehensive cultural image of *gyűlöletbeszéd* as a type of talk. Cultural discourse analysis suggests that the best way to accomplish this is by attending to four dimensions of a cultural term for communicative conduct: its relative degree of directness/indirectness (mode), the degree of restriction placed on its proper enactment (relative degree of code structuring), its emotional pitch (tone), and its perceived social consequentiality (efficacy).

Is an (alleged) act of hate speech directly addressed to a target? It is difficult to determine whether "hate speech" was seen as a direct or indirect mode of communication. In target-oriented interpretations of hate speech, a target (group) is directly affected because public hate speech renders them fearful. Audience-oriented interpretations, in contrast, suggest that an incensed audience captivated by a speaker's hate speech is responsible for the harm resulting from such speech. The audience, in this sense, functions as an intermediary between the speech and its effect on targets; thus we are presented with an image of hate speech as an indirect mode of communication.

Speaker-, target-, audience-, message-, and event-oriented act-level interpretations give us a sense of Hungarian hate speech as a type of talk with a high *degree of structuring*. Hate speech comes across as a relatively inflexible communicative practice that requires all five components (speaker, target, audience, message, event) to be present in such public talk. It is further implied that all participants must conduct themselves in specific ways (the speaker must carefully design their message, the target and the audience must respond emotionally, etc.) in order for hate speech proper to occur.

Hungarians hold strong views about the *tone* of hate speech as a type of public expression, and the tone of the target's and the audience's responses to hate speech. Some point out that hate speech is charged with the emotion of irrational prejudice against the target group. Others locate the emotional charge of hate speech in the trepidation the targets of such speech experience, or in audiences incensed by someone speaking hate speech to them. Note that, removed from the context of its use, the term "hate speech" itself hides the full range of these interpretations by seemingly locating "hatred" in the speaker or his or her speech. As we will see in the next chapter, this feature of the term leads to heated debates about the criteria one ought to use to identify hate speech.

Finally, those who are concerned about hate speech as a type of actual, observable public talk see it as highly *efficacious*. Hungarians worry about hate speech because they see it as a destructive force with the potential to threaten one's identity, reputation, or moral standing. There may be widespread disagreement about who tends to suffer the destruction of such speech and what the nature of such destruction is, but the power of hate speech to cause social chaos is undisputed.

Meanings-in-Use

The terrain of meanings surveyed in this chapter is varied and complicated. At the beginning of this chapter I suggested that those who wish to participate in Hungarian public debates about hate speech must be able to navigate this terrain. Navigating a cultural terrain of meanings, however, does not require familiarity with the terrain in its entirety. It is unlikely that any Hungarian public speaker would be familiar with the full range of meanings assigned to hate speech. They need not be. What a competent public speaker must, indeed, understand is what meanings his or her own interpretation of hate speech is likely to bring into the discussion or debate. Competence, in this case, is an exercise in foresight: "In the context of this discussion/debate/deliberative encounter if I assign meaning 'X' to hate speech, my opponent is very likely to assign meaning 'Y' to the term." Navigation, therefore, is best thought of as understanding the relationship between meaning and the context of use. As Hymes wrote, "The use of a linguistic form identifies a range of meanings. A context can support a range of meanings. When a form is used in a context, it eliminates the meanings possible to that context other than those that form can signal; the context eliminates from consideration the meanings possible to the form other than those that context can support. The effective meaning depends upon the interaction of the two."[28]

The following two chapters are case studies of the use of the term "hate speech" in context. In the first case, we will see Hungarian public intellectuals debating whether *gyűlöletbeszéd* is best identified as a type of content or a type of tone. The second case features Hungarian MPs deliberating the possibility of legal sanctions against hate speech. Both cases bring into view different interpretations of hate speech, and both teach us something about how those interpretations enter the social life of those who use them, and how they take on a social life of their own as a result.

3

INTERPRETATIONS:
TONE VERSUS CONTENT

For anyone interested in the language of argument and debate, the mass media are a good place to look for material. As Deborah Tannen pointed out in *The Argument Culture*,[1] the media often act on the assumption, in the name of journalistic objectivity, that every issue has two sides. Presenting confrontation between two sides of an issue—regardless of whether that issue had one, two, or many sides—has become the hallmark of "good" (high-quality, engaging) journalism. Some media outlets, such as talk radio or televised talk shows, have developed their own communication resources that talk show hosts can use to intensify controversy between the two sides of a debate about social issues.[2]

Regardless of whether the presentation of such debate or controversy has social value is, well, open to debate. Instead of taking a position I would like to simply claim that mass-mediated language use is an important source of cultural knowledge. The media scholar Paddy Scannell argued that a defining feature of contemporary broadcast talk is that it is designed for consumption by mass audiences whose members desire to be spoken to as members of a public *and* as individuals. Broadcast talk is a specialized kind of communication that creates the experience of "a public, shared, and sociable world-in-common between human beings,"[3] in which the individual audience member can participate as an individual. The media provide audience members with a range of concerns *and* with ways of talking about those concerns with other audience members in an intelligible and engaging manner. Contemporary broadcast talk is designed to foster social interaction.

An issue that seems to captivate mass media audiences from time to time is the question of proper participation in public discourse. (The extensive discussion of "civility" in public life in the U.S. media following the 2011 shooting of Congresswoman Gabrielle Giffords comes to mind as an example.) Scannell's theory suggests that perhaps the reason why hate speech was a favored topic of discussion in the media during the debates in Hungary was that audience members found it easy to engage with it as an issue of concern and, through the issue, with one another. The presence of a topic in broadcast talk is a good indicator that it has captured the public imagination as an issue. Hence the cultural analyst can be relatively certain that broadcast talk about the issue will be culturally meaningful (because it must feed into social interaction among audience members) and morally charged (because it tends to turn issues into debates between "sides").

Agonistic Discourse

What follows is a case study of a media event that invited reflection and commentary from a wide range of social actors in Hungary. During my years of studying *gyűlöletbeszéd* in Hungary I had become convinced that this event could be understood as a coherent, bounded illustration of the clash between two widely recognized and culturally significant interpretations of the concept. As an ethnographer, I believe that the careful study of controversies like this one can yield valuable cultural knowledge because controversies force participants to lay bare their assumptions and reasoning about how the world around them works. Case studies allow us to look two ways at the same time. We can gaze deep into the cultural systems of meaning that participants of the case rely on, and we can glance sideways toward other case studies and cultural analyses and understand the case in relation to them.

The media event I investigate in this chapter began with a radio broadcast on the Budapest radio station Klub Rádió on September 2, 2004, and spilled over into print journalism with the publication of eleven articles in the Hungarian political and literary weekly *Élet és Irodalom* (Life and literature), a publication commonly associated with the Hungarian liberal left. The series of articles, which was concluded in November 2004, further amplified the debate between two intellectual "camps" identified in the broadcast. A focal point of contention between them was whether hate speech was primarily characterized by its *hangnem* (tone) or *tartalom* (content).[4] Participants used these interpretations of *gyűlöletbeszéd* not only to take sides in the debate but also to formulate moral stances toward the concept itself.

What can the competing interpretations of an issue and its name teach us about the issue, about the participants in the competition, and about the participants' community? Sooner or later, the choice to treat the term "hate speech" as a key symbol circulating in Hungarian public discourse requires the cultural analyst to reflect on two core functions of communication: it organizes individual experience and facilitates the individual's participation in communal life.[5] When the individual speaker uses a key symbolic term in front of others, the term will point to a culturally specific system of meaning *and* a social role the individual occupies (or wishes to occupy) in a given community of speakers. Symbolic terms sometimes invoke opposing clusters of meaning within the discursive system of the speech community.[6] The opposing clusters create agonistic discourse, a way of speaking that members of a given cultural community see as presenting irreconcilable, conflicting worldviews. The formation of agonistic discourses, in turn, creates opportunities for speakers to step into social personae made relevant by the semantic opposition.[7] Such oppositions are the very foundation of much contemporary public discourse: it is possible to talk like a conservative (as opposed to a liberal), a pro-choice (as opposed to a pro-life) advocate, or a supporter of public transportation (as opposed to a supporter of the car industry). Once a speaker chooses a model of identity offered to him or her by agonistic discourse, the discourse also "tells" the speaker how the identity can be used to relate to other relevant identities.

Such a sociocultural view of contested meaning helps us imagine public discourse as enabled and constrained by the discursive system in which the speech occurs. It may also bring to mind the spectacle that is professional wrestling. The actual "fight" between two wrestlers, the trash talk, the jumping from ropes and the walloping of one's opponent with highly breakable pieces of furniture, is only half the battle. The other half is the intricate saga in which the "fighters" are cast and recast. For the wrestling fan, every move a particular wrestler makes speaks to his or her role in that saga. A similar kind of relationship exists between agonistic discourse and agonistic identities. The discourse makes sense against the backdrop of a limited set of identities and the ever-changing relationships that exist among them, and a given identity comes to life when a speaker enacts it through the creative use of language. Public debates about an issue and the words used to name, describe, and evaluate that issue teach us about the cast of public characters in a community of speakers and the story into which that community weaves those characters.

Ethnographers of communication have a continued interest in studying the relationship between conflicting ways of speaking about issues in public and the types of public identities into which they breathe life. Carbaugh[8] showed how speakers on the *Donahue* talk show engage in what he refers to as a "vacillating form of identity talk"[9] by stepping in and out of gendered identities and the universal identity of the individual as they discuss controversial issues. The vacillation occurs when participants are making strategic decisions about which identity they should occupy in the moment. Philipsen[10] contrasted identities associated with a mainstream U.S. code of dignity with identities formed within a code of honor active in a working-class, multiethnic neighborhood of Chicago. Coutu[11] tracked public responses to Robert McNamara's controversial book *In Retrospect* and identified conflicting identities formed according to a code of rationality (used by McNamara) and a code of spirituality (active in criticism targeting McNamara for his decision to support the escalation of the Vietnam War).

The Content Versus Tone Debate

Participants of the "tone" versus "content" debate in the Hungarian media were genuinely concerned about the correct definition and the distinctive features of *gyűlöletbeszéd*. But they were also concerned about managing their identities through promoting particular interpretations of the term, and particular histories of those interpretations. Arguing over the meaning of hotly contested terms in public is likely to be strategic social action designed to separate one group from another, to elevate one group onto a higher plane of morality, and to present that group as the guardian of social order.[12] The case of the tone versus content debate illustrates this process well.

In the broadcast part of the debate, the host (media personality and writer György Bolgár) and the caller (historian András Gerő) discussed Gerő's position on hate speech. This point of view was anathema to many on the Hungarian left. Gerő had argued that editorials and opinion pieces in the liberal weekly *Élet és Irodalom* (known to readers as *ÉS*) were often instances of hate speech, and compared the opinion section of *ÉS* to another publication, the *Demokrata* (The democrat), a weekly publication commonly associated with the radical right. The call was initiated by Gerő, who wished to elaborate his position on Bolgár's radio program, *Megbeszéljük* (Let's talk about it). Prior to the segment presented in excerpt 3.1, Gerő explained that both *Demokrata* and *ÉS* publish text that qualified as hate speech. In excerpts 3.1 and 3.2, Bolgár and Gerő introduced the two key symbols (tone and content) around which the agonistic discourse at the heart of this debate was organized.

Excerpt 3.1

GERŐ: Egyet kell tisztán látni. Ha tartalmi alapon közelítjük meg a gyűlöletbeszédet, akkor mindig találunk érveket arra, hogy miért helyes és indokolt. Mert gyűlöljük a fasisztákat, tehát indokolt a gyűlöletbeszéd. Mert gyűlöljük a kommunistákat, és ezért indokolt a gyűlöletbeszéd. Én meg azt mondom, hogy maga a gyűlöletbeszéd használata mindig a kritizált fél szimbolikus vagy tényleges kiiktatására, kirekesztésére szolgál. A vélt igazság nevében alkalmazott gyűlöletbeszéd mindig igazságtalansághoz vezet. Nem származás kell ehhez, nem csak származási alapon lehet valakit kirekeszteni. Hát ne haragudj, én jól emlékszem arra, amikor te megjelentettél egy regényt, aminek erősen erotikus tartalma volt és azt írta mondjuk az *ÉS*, hogy innentől a Bolgár Györggyel nem lehet szóba állni és gyakorlatilag meg kell fosztani az egzisztenciájától. Nem szabad vele szerepelni.

We must see one thing clearly. If we approach hate speech as content we will always be able to find support for why it is correct and justifiable. One can say: Because I hate fascists, hate speech is justifiable. Because I hate Communists, hate speech is justifiable. And I say that the use of hate speech itself serves the symbolic or actual elimination or discrimination of the critiqued party. The use of hate speech in the name of an assumed truth always leads to injustice. It is not ethnicity that matters, discrimination can happen not just on the basis of ethnicity. I'm sorry but I do remember when you [Bolgár] published a novel that featured explicitly erotic content, and it was *ÉS* that said from now on no one should talk to György Bolgár and that he should be practically stripped of his livelihood. One shouldn't publicly associate with him.[13]

Gerő introduces his central argument about the pitfall of identifying hate speech as "content." If we view it thus, Gerő argues, we provide speakers of hate speech, including some journalists writing for *ÉS* and others, with an opportunity to justify their own hate speech as the expression of a kind of righteous indignation toward hateful targets. This interpretation, Gerő maintains, allows these speakers not only to cast their hate speech as the morally charged critique of fascists or communists, but also to eliminate them, which, as an act of "discrimination," is an instance of "injustice."

Then Gerő poses a subtle challenge to Bolgár. Since Bolgár was the object of "symbolic or actual elimination" by *ÉS* for the erotic "content" of his novel, Gerő argues, Bolgár cannot maintain that the weekly should not be held accountable for hate speech. This move has the potential to undermine Bolgár's identity as a public figure representing a clear and consistent position on hate speech. In excerpt 3.2, Bolgár responds to Gerő's challenge with a partial concession and two types of counter-challenge: tacitly charging Gerő with hate speech and specifying what kind of content qualifies as such.

Excerpt 3.2

BOLGÁR: Na, jó, hogy ezt szóba hozod, mert valóban rosszul esett nekem, igazságtalannak is tartottam, de ettől én még mindig nem vagyok hajlandó az *Élet és Irodalmat* kirekeszteni, és azt mondani rá, hogy a gyűlöletbeszéd rendszeresen megjelenik ott. Legfeljebb azt mondom, hogy indulatos, adott esetben akár még gyűlölettel teli és igazságtalan vélemények is megfogalmazódnak benne. Jó, adott esetben még velem szemben is. Ettől a lap még nem kívánja sem a kommunista diktatúra, sem a fasiszta diktatúra vagy a nyilas diktatúra visszatérését. Ezt szellemileg nem készíti elő, sőt valamiféle ideális demokráciában szeretne élni. Néha ezért is erősebb és kirekesztőbb a hangneme talán, mint másoké.

GERŐ: Nézd, itt valószínű érdemi különbség van az álláspontok között. Én, mint jeleztem az előbb, először is nem a lap egészéről beszéltem, hanem a publicisztika meghatározó hangneméről.

BOLGÁR: Well, I'm glad you mention that because I was hurt then, and I thought it was unjust, but I still refuse to discriminate against *Élet és Irodalom* and say that it publishes hate speech on a regular basis. The most I am willing to say is that temperamental, or in some cases even hateful and unjust opinions are formulated in it. OK, in some cases even against me. But that does not mean that the paper longs for the return of the communist dictatorship or the Arrow Cross dictatorship.[14] Not only is it not making an intellectual effort to prepare their return, it wants to exist in some kind of ideal democracy. Because of that it uses perhaps a stronger and more discriminatory tone than others.

GERŐ: Look, I think we have a substantial difference of views here. As I have indicated before, I am not talking about the paper as a whole but about the dominant tone of the opinion pieces.[15]

Bolgár accepts that the attacks against him by *ÉS* were "hurtful" and "unjust." He adds that "in some cases even hateful and unjust opinions are formulated in [the weekly]." Thus he acknowledges that "tone" is a defining characteristic of the opinion pieces he and Gerő are discussing. After these concessions, however, he launches a double challenge against Gerő. First, he applies an act-level interpretation of hate speech—discrimination—to characterize Gerő's stance against *ÉS* by saying that he himself "refuse[s] to discriminate against *Élet és Irodalom* and say that it publishes hate speech on a regular basis." In the role of third-party judge, he casts Gerő's charge of hate speech against the weekly as itself an instance of hate speech—a discursive move not uncommon in Hungarian public debates on the issue.[16] Next, he highlights that a type of content, an essential component of hate speech, is conspicuously missing from *ÉS*: "The paper [does not long] for the return of the communist dictatorship or the Arrow Cross dictatorship. . . . [It is] not making an intellectual effort to prepare their return." By specifying the type of content that transforms public speech into hate speech, Bolgár accomplishes three things: he calls into question Gerő's position, he makes the argument that content rather than tone is a decisive indicator of hate speech, and he maintains his identity as a well-informed, reasonable person with a nuanced take on the issue.

Bolgár's interpretation points to a culturally relevant difference between speech voiced with the tone of hatred (i.e., it is aggressive or vitriolic) and speech that is hateful because it represents communist or national socialist ideology. He further argues that in the case of *ÉS*, "a stronger and more discriminatory tone" in fact serves the advent of "ideal democracy," which stands in opposition with political ideologies inspiring real hate speech. In Gerő's response, we see that the two have reached a stalemate regarding their interpretations of hate speech. Gerő characterizes their opposing interpretive stances as "a substantial difference of views" and adopts the tone-oriented interpretation as his own.

Two Controversial Aspects of the Debate: Semantic History and Affect

Besides elaborating the two sides of the debate,[17] the articles in *ÉS* published during the two months after the broadcast assigned different semantic histories to the term "hate speech." They also differed on whether emotion was one of its defining characteristics. Let's have a look at history first as a dimension of the debate that seemed especially significant from the participants' perspective. Those arguing for the content orientation leaned toward interpreting the migration of hate speech from U.S. political discourse into Hungarian usage as the mutation and loss of meaning. Advocates of the tone orientation, the clear minority, described this history as the inevitable transformation of the term's meaning to reflect Hungarians' social experiences. The following two excerpts, from articles written by the Hungarian philosopher Gáspár Miklós Tamás (3.3) and András Gerő (3.4), illustrate these two histories.

Excerpt 3.3

A magyarországi politikai viták egyik nehézsége—elsősorban 1989 óta— hogy a Nyugatról átvett fogalmak különös változásokon mennek keresztül:

szemantikai, kulturális, szociológiai, konnotációs változásokon. Ez elég természetes, mégis bosszúságokat okoz, mert némelyek az eredeti nyugati (elfogadott, kodifikált) jelentésükben használják a szakkifejezéseket, mások meg nem. . . .

Ugyanez lett a sorsa a "gyűlöletbeszéd" kifejezésnek Magyarországon. A hate speech, amely szakkifejezés (*terminus technicus*), az amerikai egyetemi campusok egyik belső, pedagógiai és politikai célzatú stratégiáját jelöli. Mivel az Egyesült Államokban korlátlan a sajtószabadság (szemben a legtöbb európai országgal, beleértve Nyugat-Európát), ezért az egyetemeken önszabályozást kellett bevezetni, amely megvédi a faji-etnikai kisebbségekhez tartozó (elsősorban fekete és bevándorló/külföldi), meleg, leszbikus, transzszexuális, fogyatékkal élő, beteg, szegény diákokat—és persze a diáklányokat—a verbális zaklatástól, bántástól, szomorítástól. Ezért az egyetemek tilalmazták az effélét, és fegyelmi eljárás alá vonták a speech code (a megengedhető beszéd kódjának) mindenekelőtt rasszista és szexista megsértőit. . . .

A "gyűlöletbeszéd" tehát nem a beszéd tónusára vonatkozik, nem a "hangnem"-re, hanem bizonyos tartalmakra. A "gyűlöletbeszéd" a kisebbségek és a (valamilyen szempontból) idegenek ellen irányuló beszéd, és nem kell hevesnek vagy gorombának lennie.

One of the difficulties that has plagued political debates, especially since 1989,[18] is that concepts adopted from the West undergo peculiar changes, semantic, cultural, sociological, connotational changes. This is quite natural yet also disconcerting because some use these technical terms according to their original (accepted, codified) meaning, and others do not. . . .

The term "gyűlöletbeszéd" had met a similar fate in Hungary. The technical term (*terminus technicus*) "hate speech" denotes an internal, pedagogically and politically oriented strategy on U.S. university campuses. Since in the United States there is a complete freedom of the press (as opposed to most European countries, including western Europe), universities were required to introduce self-regulation that protects racial/ethnic minority (primarily black and immigrant/foreign), gay, lesbian, transsexual, disabled, sick, and poor students (and, of course, female students)[19] from verbal harassment, harm, and emotional abuse. To this end, universities had outlawed such conduct and subjected, first and foremost, the racist and sexist offenders of the "speech code" (the code of acceptable speech) to disciplinary proceedings. . . .

"Gyűlöletbeszéd" therefore does not refer to the style of speech, nor to its "tone," but to specific types of content. "Gyűlöletbeszéd" is speech directed against minorities and outsiders (of any kind). Such speech does not need to be agitated or rude [to qualify as hate speech].[20]

Tamás locates the meaning of hate speech in a U.S. content-oriented interpretation. Within the framework of this "strategy," hate speech as a "technical term" has an authoritative ("accepted, codified") interpretation. The source of this authority is the legal vocabulary of the original U.S. campus speech codes. When removed from this context, the term becomes subject to "semantic, cultural, sociological, connotational changes." This is a natural but unfortunate process, Tamás argues, which can result in the loss of original meaning. Such loss is exemplified by the reference to "hate speech" as "tone."

The tone camp punctuates this semantic history in a different way. For them, the origin of the term is the same (the United States), but the source of authority determining the meaning of the term is contemporary Hungarian social experience.

Excerpt 3.4

A gyűlöletbeszéd kategóriája viszonylag új keletű, s mint az minden új fogalom esetében megfigyelhető, a tartalom még nem teljesen letisztult. Eredetileg—az USA-ban—főként a rasszista tartalomra használták, s napjainkban jelentése tovább dúsult. Lassan beleértődik mindaz, ami diszkriminatív, esetleg lekezelő a nemi, illetve különféle kisebbségi csoportokkal szemben—s itt a kisebbség szó nem feltétlenül statisztikai kategória. (A nők például számszerű többséget alkotnak—ettől azonban a szexista tartalmú beszéd még sújthatja őket.)

A fogalom amerikai tartalma esetében is alapvető szempont az, hogy elsődlegesen azokról szól, akiket különféle okok miatt hátrányos megkülönböztetés ért vagy ér. Teljesen magától értetődnek és természetesnek gondolom, hogy a fogalom minden kultúrában részben átértelmeződik, és azokkal a társadalmi tapasztalati anyagokkal töltődik fel, amelyek élénken beépültek egy közösség emlékezetébe. . . .

Tehát a gyűlöletbeszéd valóban tartalmi kategória, de tartalmát az adott társadalom élményanyaga tölti fel. Az élményanyagot pedig az hitelesíti, hogy az emberek tudják: melyik narratíva mihez vezetett. Félelmeiket, érzékelésüket is ez szabja meg. Magyarországon soha nem lesz oly félelmetes az egyébként helytelen szexista beszéd, mint a zsidózás vagy a politikai ellenségképgyártás. Magyarországon a politikai gyűlöletbeszéd mintegy szintetizáló módon építette magába a lehetséges félelmek és jogfosztások teljes tárházát s ez milliók élményévé vált.

The category of hate speech is relatively new, and as it can be observed in the case of any new concept its meaning is not yet completely clear. In the USA, it was originally applied chiefly to racist content and its meaning has become richer. Gradually it came to encompass everything that is discriminatory or perhaps demeaning toward sexual or other minority groups; here, minorities are not necessarily a statistical category. (For example, women constitute a numeric majority, which does not mean that they cannot be subjected to sexist speech.)

A basic consideration implied in the American use of the concept as well is that it addresses the situation of those who suffered or continue to suffer from discrimination for a variety of reasons. I think it is completely self-evident and natural that the concept would acquire new meaning in all cultures and become charged with social experience living a vivid life in the memory of a given community. . . .

Therefore, hate speech is indeed a type of content, but that content is derived from the totality of a given society's experiences. What lends credibility to this totality of experience is the fact that people know which narrative leads to what event. Their fears and perceptions are determined by the same knowledge. In Hungary, inappropriate sexist speech will never be considered as fearsome as *zsidózás* [making derogatory references or allusions to Jews] or the construction of political enemies. In Hungary, political hate speech had absorbed and synthesized the complete repository of all possible fears and acts of disenfranchisement, and this became the experience of millions.[21]

Gerő paints a different picture of the concept's history. The meaning of the term passed through an original phase in which its meaning was restricted to "racist content." Next, its meaning has become "richer," as in contemporary times it gradually "came to encompass everything that is discriminatory or perhaps demeaning toward sexual or other minority groups." Finally, running separately from, but parallel with, this second phase is a third phase in which "the concept would acquire new meaning in all cultures and become charged with social experience living a vivid life in the memory of a given community." This third phase gave rise to the development of "political hate speech," which includes at least two kinds of communicative acts: "*zsidózás* [making derogatory references or allusions to Jews]" and "the construction of political enemies."

Did Gerő change his mind about hate speech as defined by tone? The phrase "hate speech is indeed a type of content" certainly seems to imply a shift in his position. This is, however, not the case. What Gerő is attempting to accomplish in his article is the articulation *and* straddling of the tone–content dichotomy. It is useful to spend some time reviewing his argument because it offers insight into a specifically Hungarian interpretation of hate speech.

The key to Gerő's interpretation is the symbolic terms for the "construction of political enemies" or "political hate speech." Hungary's twentieth-century history, Gerő explains in the article, was overshadowed by two political dictatorships. The first of these, fascism, tainted the political right; the second, communism, corrupted the political left. In political debates in the Hungarian context, stigmatizing references to the opponent are frequently made in the radical politicking of right- and left-wing journalists whose work is often published in the *Demokrata* and *ÉS*. Most of this work is marked by a style that Gerő calls *mocskolódás* (smearing), the objective of which is to vilify persons, and destroy their reputation and, potentially, their livelihood. In a previously discussed excerpt, Gerő referred to this type of communicative action as the "symbolic or actual elimination or discrimination of the critiqued party." Although smearing is a style of personal attack with a particular tone, in the Hungarian political context this tone becomes the vehicle of the stigmatizing logic of political *gyűlöletbeszéd*. Thus the speech referred to as smearing is also a candidate for hate speech because it presumes and ignites existing hatred against the opposing political faction. The smeared person stands in for a stigmatized political group or a political side, left or right. Persons castigated for their affiliation with the right are discursively transformed into Nazi or fascist sympathizers, while persons with leftist ties are turned into friends of communists. Under special historical and political circumstances, tone can *interact* with hateful content to form hate speech. Smearing does not necessarily evolve into hate speech, however, and hateful content can constitute hate speech even without a hateful tone.

This type of hate speech, Gerő explains, leaves room for types that are less specific to the Hungarian context, such as racist or sexist speech. These latter, more universal types of hate speech, however, cannot be as "fearsome" as anti-Semitic talk or political hate speech because they do not reflect what Gerő refers to at a different point of the article as Hungarian "hate narratives."[22] Such narratives include historical accounts of deportations of former aristocrats during communist times, and anti-Semitic laws gradually introduced from the 1920s through the early 1940s. These narratives in Hungarian public discourse fuel fear by lending credibility to Hungarians' fear of potential future persecution: "People know which narrative leads to what event. Their fears and perceptions are determined by the same knowledge."

Let us return to the broadcast discussed at the beginning of this chapter to investigate participants' concern with whether the speaker's feelings were a key characteristic of hate speech. Besides providing clues about participants' interpretations of the relation between emotion and hate speech, excerpt 3.5 is also an illustration of two interpretations of the concept that participants see as irreconcilable.

Excerpt 3.5

BOLGÁR: De a gyűlöletbeszéden te azt érted, hogy esetleg gyűlölnek téged, vagy gyűlölnek engem, miközben leírják a kritikájukat, ami esetleg emberi hiba, vagy indulat, vagy akárminek nevezzük, vagy pedig azt, hogy szisztematikusan kirekesztők, szisztematikusan mondjuk származási alapon megkülönböztetik a társadalom egyes csoportjait és ennek megfelelő társadalompolitikai, etikai, filozófiai következtetéseket vonnak le?

GERŐ: Válasszunk ketté két dolgot. A gyűlölet mint érzet az ember legsajátabb énjéhez tartozik. Attól vagyunk emberek, hogy vannak érzelmeink, adott esetben gyűlöletnek is hívhatjuk ezt az érzelmet. Ezt természetesnek tartom, emberinek tartom. Ami azonban minden társadalmat és minden kultúrát jellemez, hogy az ösztönös érzelmi világot milyen kulturális formákban hagyja kibontakozni. Hadd mondjak egy analógiát. Minden emberben ott működik a szexuális ösztön, de mégis, kulturálisan rendkívül szabályozott, hogy nyilvános térben mit enged meg kifejezésképpen és mit nem ez az ösztön. Ugyanígy van a gyűlölettel is. A gyűlölet elfogadható, emberi. A gyűlöletbeszéd az én álláspontom szerint elfogadhatatlan.

BOLGÁR: Na de miért gyűlöletbeszéd az, hogy ha az *Élet és Irodalomban* mondjuk, néha tegyük fel, gyűlölettel átitatott írás is megjelenik, és miért ugyanaz ez, mint a *Demokratában* szisztematikusan, rendszeresen megjelenő olyan cikkek, amelyekkel rehabilitálják még a Szálasi-korszakot is, vagy kétségbe vonják azt, hogy Auschwitzban gázkamrák voltak.

BOLGÁR: But when you say hate speech do you mean that they hate you or they hate me as they write their critiques, which is human fallibility or passion or what have you, or do you mean that they systematically discriminate, they treat certain groups in society differently on the basis of, say, their ethnicity and arrive at matching sociopolitical, ethical, or philosophical conclusions?

GERŐ: Let us distinguish two things. As an emotion, hatred belongs to humans' core selves. We are humans because we have feelings. Let's take hatred for the purpose of this discussion. I consider this natural and human. However, every society and every culture is characterized by the cultural forms that they use when they allow manifestations of the instinctive emotional world. Let me use an analogy. A sexual instinct is at work in every human being. Still, how that instinct is expressed in the public sphere is culturally regulated to a great extent. The same thing with hatred. Hatred is acceptable, human. Hate speech, in my view, is unacceptable.

BOLGÁR: Well, but why is it hate speech when in *Élet és Irodalom*, sometimes, let's say, an article appears that is suffused with hatred, and why is that the same thing as those articles published systematically, regularly in *Demokrata* that rehabilitate even the Szálasi era or call into question whether there indeed were gas chambers in Auschwitz?[23]

In the first turn, Bolgár presents Gerő with two interpretive choices that he frames as mutually exclusive: conceiving of hate speech as "human fallibility, or passion," or as a communicative act that "systematically discriminate[s] . . . on the basis of . . . [a given social group's] ethnicity." In response, Gerő locates the source of hatred as an emotion in "humans' core selves," and contrasts emotion with "cultural form that [societies] use when they allow manifestations of the instinctual emotional world." Culture is capable of regulating the emotion of hatred, just as it can regulate natural "sexual instinct." Culture, as Gerő uses it here, is reminiscent of German *Kultur*, a vision of culture as the ethereal realm of high forms of public expression, such as art and philosophy. Such expression is imagined as unblemished by raw instinct and emotion, although capable of sublimating these into an idealized form. In hate speech, the ugly, unrestrained emotion of hatred bubbles from the core self into the public sphere without taking on a cultural form. Without regulation and restraint, even though hatred as part of human nature is "acceptable," hate speech is to be understood as "unacceptable" public expression. The presentation of hate speech as public expression lacking in civility is a token of the tone-based interpretation.

After Gerő's turn, Bolgár upholds the distinction between hatred as an emotional form of expression and as a systematic, regular form of expression intended to "rehabilitate the Szálasi era or call into question whether there indeed were gas chambers in Auschwitz." There is an important distinction to be made, Bolgár says, between passionate speech marked by hatred, and hate speech as systematic, regular action or the expression of ideological content associated with fascism and the Holocaust.

"Hate Speech" and Its Consequences

Neither side of the content–tone debate would deny that *gyűlöletbeszéd* threatens Hungarian society. However, the ways they identify the nature of the threat and its antidote differed. The content perspective posits a three-pronged threat. First, hate speech as an act is used to express and bring about discrimination and the differential treatment of social groups "on the basis of, say, their ethnicity." Second, perpetrators of hate speech base their actions on a coherent body of theoretical considerations as they "arrive at matching sociopolitical, ethical, or philosophical conclusions." These conclusions lead them to assign positive value to Hungary's fascist past, and to "question whether there indeed were gas chambers in Auschwitz." Third, as Bolgár says in a part of the broadcast conversation I haven't included in this chapter, hate speech feeds into the "intellectual founding of the return of a system that disappeared sixty years ago, a return we all thought was impossible today, in a democratic environment" (szellemi megalapozása folyik annak a hatvan évvel ezelott letűnt rendszer visszahozatalának, amiről úgy gondoltuk, hogy ma már a demokratikus környezetben lehetetlen). Hate speech as ethnic discrimination is linked directly to the threat of the return of a particularly dark period in Hungary's history.

The interpretation of hate speech as tone implies that it threatens society by releasing unregulated hatred into the public sphere. "That is so," Gerő explains to Bolgár at a different point of their discussion, "because the people who have a vested interest in hate speech, and whose only currency is not intellectual argument but the use of hatred itself, become capable of setting both the agenda and style of public expression" (Mert ezáltal azok az emberek, akik a gyűlöletbeszédben érdekeltek, és egyetlen fizetőeszközük nem az intellektuális mondandó, hanem maga a gyűlölet használata, képessé válnak a közbeszéd tematizálására s arra, hogy megszabják annak stílusát). Hate speech therefore does not only inject hateful content into the public sphere, it also sets the style (or tone) of public engagement.

Different threats require different antidotes. From the content perspective, *ÉS* journalists' desire "to exist in some kind of ideal democracy," and their use of "a stronger and more discriminatory tone" toward that end, is commendable. By implication, an effective way to act against hate speech as content is the use of a passionate tone against such speakers. As another participant in the debate put it, "Nazism cannot be hated without hatred for Nazis" (A nácizmust sem lehet gyűlölni a nácik gyűlölete nélkül).[24] By contrast, the tone orientation calls for the use of "intellectual argument" in the public sphere. The proposed antidote is a type of rational style with the potential to cleanse public discourse of hate speech.

Verbal Hygiene

Cultural thinking about this polarized and polarizing debate teaches us three things about public participation. First, the tone versus content debate is not a mere intellectual exercise but an agonistic discourse charged with morality and identity concerns.[25] This is hardly a uniquely Hungarian phenomenon. A cultural analysis of the interaction between faculty members and administrators at a U.S. university yielded similar insights.[26] The two sides failed to agree on whether "talking things through" or "putting them in writing" was the best way to deal with problems and dilemmas associated with operating an institute of higher education. Administrators and faculty

> failed to frame their governance dispute in terms of discrepant commu-
> nication codes, electing instead to engage in discursive assertions and
> counter-assertions that proclaimed the superiority of their own governance
> model and which caricatured members of the competing code community
> through a variety of negative dispositional attributes. . . . Thus, members
> of the two code communities resorted to what Bailey (1983) describes as
> "the rhetoric of assertion," that is, emotive assertions of moral superiority
> designed less to promote reasoned dialogue with competing factions and
> more to bolster the "true believers" of one's own faction and to provoke
> emotional attachment from the uncommitted.[27]

Second, controversies featuring agonistic discourse sometimes play out with reference to other controversies. Such interactions between controversies may amplify the moral charge of agonistic discourse. Some participants in the tone versus content debate invoked another ongoing public debate surrounding András Gerő's decision to work closely with the controversial conservative historian Mária Schmidt. Gerő was declared "lost"[28] and an apologist for *Demokrata*, a "neo-Nazi fanzine"[29] whose tone Gerő compared to that of op-eds in *ÉS*. Others[30] entered the fray supporting Gerő, who characterized his opponents as the "homegrown writers" (*háziszerző*) of *ÉS*.[31]

Finally, the cultural analysis of the debate illustrated that although controversy about hot-button issues can tear the social fabric of a community of speakers, it does not necessarily lead to a lack of understanding between the two sides. The tone-based interpretation of hate speech remained intelligible, even partially acceptable, to those advocating the content-based interpretation, and vice versa. Lack of understanding was not the issue—participants were concerned about the social and moral consequences of advocating and endorsing particular interpretations of hate speech over others. The tone versus content debate reminds us forcefully that the cultural meaning of language is to be found not in words, phrases, and sentences but in communal members' strategic use of words, phrases, and sentences.

One of the most astute analysts and critics of language's life in public, Deborah Cameron, helps us construct a comprehensive image of the debate over interpretations of hate speech as social action. In *Verbal Hygiene*,[32] Cameron studies the social practice of symbolically cleansing public discourse of elements the verbal hygienist finds objectionable. These elements include any phenomenon of language use that verbal hygienists hold to be nonnormative and therefore value negatively. Syntax, dialect, and various forms and tropes of political expression are all fair game. By assigning normative status to specific kinds of uses, verbal hygienists infuse those uses with superior moral value and authority. Consequently, nonnormative use is framed as a breach of the social contract that will likely lead to the breakdown of social coherence: "Debates on verbal hygiene are of particular interest [because] conflict renders visible the processes of norm-making and norm-breaking, bringing into the open the arguments that surround rules."[33] The tone versus content debate as agonistic discourse can be productively framed as a sometimes amicable, sometimes aggressive confrontation between rival camps of verbal hygienists. Their interpretations may have been different but their goals were the same: to identify hate speech that Hungarian society must be purged of, to argue for the necessity of purging, and to identify the most effective way to accomplish the purge. Verbal hygiene in this debate is concerned explicitly with the moral implications of *gyűlöletbeszéd* as communicative action.

Moral struggles in public are also political struggles. Verbal hygienists recognize that the public judgment of public expression is a political act. Occupying a position of moral authority allows one to shape others' judgments about what public uses of language should be assigned normative status. A verbal hygienist in the position of moral authority can also legitimately identify speakers who use language in a nonnormative manner and present these speakers as "bad subjects"[34] who, having violated the social contract, pose a danger to social integrity.

Identifying, condemning, and sanctioning hate speech are at once moral and political acts in the social drama of a nation emerging from decades of authoritarian rule. This chapter demonstrated cultural thinking about identification and condemnation; the following chapter, the case study of deliberation in the Hungarian Parliament about legislative measures against hate speech, continues these themes but develops a stronger focus on the act of sanctioning.

4

INTERPRETATIONS:

HOW TO SANCTION "HATE SPEECH"

Most of us are not used to thinking about the law as something "cultural." In fact, we like to think of the law as an entirely culture-free system of social controls that shapes the lives of all citizens without regard to their culture, race, or ethnicity. But, as with everything humans do, law and lawmaking can also be made the subject of cultural thinking. Geertz teaches us that any particular legal system can be looked at as the answer of particular communities to the question of how to lead principled lives in practicable ways.[1] The language of the law mediates between a community's vision of what everyday life should be like and legal decision making in specific cases of dispute. The social power of law, Geertz says, results from the fact that the language of the law renders specific rulings within the context of a given legal system sensible to members of society.

In this second case study I demonstrate how a specific genre of political action (debate over the language of law) brings into view culture (different versions of imagined social reality). More specifically, I take a cultural look at Hungarian lawmakers as they negotiate the meaning of "free expression" and "hate speech" in the process of debating a proposed piece of legislation designed to outlaw "provocation to hatred." The limits of free expression have been the subject of legal battles throughout the Western world for centuries. Cultural thinking compels us to assume that such disputes must be rooted, at least in part, in conflicting beliefs about how the world works. To better understand the cultural interpretations that feed into the language of Hungarian law about free expression, I take readers to one source of the law: the chambers of the Hungarian Parliament.

Communal Meanings of Freedom of Speech

The study of free expression and hate speech I present here joins a limited but increasing number of others that base their arguments about the social function of free expression on field research. Field-based studies often end up advocating one of two seemingly irreconcilable arguments: that local worldview (including the local moral system) *should* determine local legal practice, or that local legal practice *should* determine the local worldview. The theoretical about-face made by the free speech scholar Donald Alexander Downs is a nice illustration of both these arguments. In *Nazis in Skokie*, Downs passionately critiques the content neutrality rule (i.e., that speech should not become the subject of legal sanctions on the basis of its content) in free speech adjudication.[2] The speech of National Socialist Party of America members marching through Skokie, a Chicago suburb, was clearly designed to injure the Holocaust survivors living there. As such, the NSPA directly threatened the survivors' right to autonomy and self-governance. In this book, Downs calls for limiting the freedom of expression by applying the fighting words doctrine and the concept of group libel to public speech. In his most recent book, *Restoring Free Speech and Liberty on Campus*, Downs advocates the opposite view on reverse grounds.[3] Based on a review of four cases of speech code debates on U.S. university campuses, he concludes that so-called progressives have abused harassment codes by using them to silence well-meaning professors and students. The solution, according to Downs, is that First Amendment–based legal practice outside the university ought to keep the moral cause (the protection of vulnerable groups) in check within the university. Otherwise, morally based arguments for curtailing free speech will harm innocent bystanders and will hinder free inquiry on campus. The contradiction is clear: while Downs wrote his first book to convince the reader to match law to the world, in his second book he made a case for matching the world to law.

I don't want to take issue with Downs's arguments for or against imposing legal restrictions on public expression. What I disagree with is his either-or prescriptive representation of an allegedly one-way relationship between worldview and legal practice. From a cultural perspective, the social function of law is to bring together the "picture of 'what is right' and stories of 'what is so'";[4] that is, to create a persuasive link between the ways a community makes sense of an infinitely complex world and the facts of a given case (evidence). The law sets into motion a mutually constitutive relationship between communal interpretations of appropriate conduct and local legal practice. As Downs searches for social justice for two sorts of victims in two vastly different social realms—a suburban community of Holocaust survivors and the campuses of four major U.S. research universities—he misses what is a basic fact for the ethnographer: different communities observe different norms of conduct depending on their experiences in, and the sense they make of, the world. The same law (in this case, the First

Amendment) may err on the side of morality from the vantage point of one community, and on the side of legal practice from the perspective of another. Downs's conversion is as much from communitarian to libertarian thinking about free expression as from one community's worldview to another's.

Other prescriptive studies of the significance of free expression in specific communities also tend to either advocate imposing the principles of a moral system on local legal practice, or vice versa. Nielsen's study of street harassment in urban America calls for reconsidering First Amendment absolutism from a moral perspective.[5] According to her, the current legal stance toward free expression fails to shield women and minorities from street harassment and must therefore be rethought. In their analysis of free expression in Morocco, Smith and Loudiy proceed in the opposite direction.[6] They join progressive Moroccan political activists in faulting the king of Morocco for refusing to observe the universal right to free expression on local moral and religious grounds. The king, they show, taps into traditional Moroccan beliefs about the sociocultural status of royalty when he places himself and his household outside the realm of public criticism. Once again, I do not dispute the authors' call for greater social justice in the United States and Morocco. As an ethnographer I do, however, miss cultural thinking from their arguments; I miss an interest in the cultural logic of the *existing* legal and political systems they are criticizing. They may have asked: What system of cultural assumptions makes the protection of street harassment as free speech seem plausible to many in the United States? And what cultural premises prompt many non-activist Moroccans to accept the status of the person of the king and his household as untouchable by public criticism?

The approach I use in this chapter is not without precedent. Carbaugh analyzes the communal rules of public presentations of self on the U.S. television talk show *Donahue* and argues that the American legal discourse of the "right" to free expression is deeply rooted in a local view of the world.[7] Yankah also traces the meaning of free expression in Ghana to the beliefs of traditional Ghanaian society.[8] The style of interpretation these studies adopt and that I will use here proceeds in two moves. First, it is necessary to understand what speakers mean *in what contexts* as they use terms with powerful symbolic meanings such as "free expression," "hate speech" and "human dignity." Attention to context helps the analyst understand the ways that speech plays into or shapes existing social arrangements. Second, using these symbols the analyst accounts for *cultural premises*, taken-for-granted communal assumptions about the nature of the world without which language use would be incoherent.

Talking About "Hate Speech" in the Hungarian Parliament

The standing committees of the Hungarian Parliament gather in committee meeting rooms located either in the main building of the Parliament or a few blocks away in the Representatives' Office Building, an edifice often referred to as the White House for the color of its facade. (The reference to a building of the same name in Washington, D.C., is not lost on Hungarians.) A typical meeting room contains a rectangular table in the middle of the room with chairs around it for committee members. Guests are seated on another set of chairs along the wall. The chairperson, the deputy chairperson, and a staff member in charge of the minutes and vote counts sit at one end of the table, while MPs occupy the other three sides. All committee members speak into microphones. The microphones serve both a technical and an interactional purpose. They are used to create a public record of conversations among MPs, and they also control MPs' participation in those conversations. A speaker can only claim the floor "officially" if they are the only person whose microphone is switched on. (No two microphones can be on at the same time.) The transcripts I reviewed do sometimes capture the talk of MPs whose microphone is not turned on, but these utterances are cast as unofficial interruptions since they are not licensed by the chairperson or his or her deputy.

The participants in these sittings are current MPs elected to the committees by the General Assembly. The actual composition of the parliamentary committees (i.e., the roster the General Assembly votes on) is often the result of negotiation among the political parties. Committee members usually meet on a weekly basis, and are convened by the chairperson or his or her deputy. Members can ask other MPs to serve as their proxies for a given meeting in case they are unable to attend.

Committee meetings follow a predictable sequence. The chairperson opens the meeting and presents the agenda for the day. Members can raise questions about agenda items at this point. The chairperson then reads the list of proxies and announces whether the committee has a quorum. Afterward, the chairperson introduces agenda items one by one. In some cases, the representative of the government introduces a new bill, which is then discussed. MPs can also introduce modifications to bills they sponsor. After the discussion, the committee votes on whether to support a given bill, or to pass a resolution or a statement of the committee's standpoint. If the bill receives majority support it is forwarded to the General Assembly for further debate. At the end of the meeting the chairperson usually thanks the members for their work and announces the date of the next meeting.

This chapter reconstructs the cultural logic of how MPs discussed Bill No. T/5179. In the bill, the Ministry of Justice proposed an amendment to the piece of legislation passed in 1978 (see chapter 1). The amendments were to further specify the section of the Hungarian criminal code about incitement against a community. The modified version of the law contained two new elements. It distinguished "provocation to hatred" from "calls for committing a forcible act" against national, ethnic, racial, or religious groups or their individual members, and deemed both of these criminal acts. It also characterized as criminal offense the "violation of human dignity" by "disparagement" of others on the basis of their group membership or by preaching racial, ethnic, national or religious inferiority or superiority. During the series of committee meetings in which this bill was discussed, committee members proposed a number of modifications to the modification. The bill was then forwarded to the General Assembly and turned into a final proposal. The Hungarian Constitutional Court struck down this proposal on May 24, 2004, on the grounds that it violated the freedom of opinion.

Three key communicative patterns stand out from the transcripts. First, no MP disagreed with what MP László Donáth of the Hungarian Socialist Party, a member of the Committee on Human Rights, Minorities, Civil, and Religious Affairs, had to say about hate speech: "Basically all of us agree that we must act against the practice of hate speech, any type of it and any manifestation of it against anyone."[9] Second, "violation of human dignity" was used as a key cultural symbol. At least one MP in all three committees interpreted gyűlöletbeszéd as a "violation of human dignity" (az emberi méltóság megsértése). Again, no MP spoke up to challenge this interpretation. Dr. László Soós, the government representative responsible for introducing the bill to all three committees, further supported the observation that this symbol was of paramount importance. In his introductory remarks to the Committee on Constitutional and Judicial Affairs, Soós said that the language of the newly proposed law would match previous versions by calling for the penalization of "statements" that "denigrate [or] humiliate" others by invoking racial or religious membership, or racial inferiority or superiority. It would, however, diverge from these earlier versions by penalizing these statements "as violations of human dignity" (az emberi méltóság megsértésén keresztül).[10] MPs talked about such "statements" (along with some other types) throughout the committee sittings as "hate speech." Because the "violation of human dignity" seemed to be of such concern to all MPs, I will treat this phrase as a key symbolic term and, as such, a window onto the symbolic system the committee meeting talk draws on. Third, although MPs all negatively evaluated hate speech and agreed that it constituted the violation of human dignity, committee members also agreed that these basic assumptions lead to contrasting interpretations of the Hungarian Constitution. To quote Dr. Zoltán Szabó, a member of both the Committee on Cultural Affairs and the Media and the Socialist Party, "Indeed what we are dealing with is a contradiction between fundamental constitutional rights: the right to the freedom of opinion is placed in contradiction with the right to human dignity and the right of minorities to legal security."[11]

When reading the transcripts, I was immediately intrigued by talk about this contradiction, for two reasons. The contradiction Szabó points out is one that lawmakers in most Western legal systems grapple with all the time. The contradiction can be phrased roughly as follows: if lawmakers curtail free expression (or "freedom of opinion," as it is often referred to in Hungarian), they violate a basic human right; if they do not, they become complicit in the violation of another (the right to human dignity). The other reason why my interest was piqued was that fundamental dilemmas in society take the cultural analyst to the heart of the cultural system of that society. Such dilemmas are the very reason why people feel compelled, and sometimes forced, to grapple with issues of morality, value, and belief.[12] And when people grapple with norms and beliefs, ethnographers usually have important things to say about that.

Before we turn to identifying a system of key symbols in MPs' talk, let us review those sections of the Hungarian Constitution that are relevant to their discussion and the dilemma they are confronted with.

Excerpt 4.1

54. § (1) A Magyar Köztársaságban minden embernek veleszületett joga van az élethez és az emberi méltósághoz, amelyektől senkit nem lehet önkényesen megfosztani. . . .

61. § (1) A Magyar Köztársaságban mindenkinek joga van a szabad véleménynyilvánításra, továbbá arra, hogy a közérdekű adatokat megismerje, illetőleg terjessze. . . .

70/A. § (1) A Magyar Köztársaság biztosítja a területén tartózkodó minden személy számára az emberi, illetve az állampolgári jogokat, bármely megkülönböztetés, nevezetesen faj, szín, nem, nyelv, vallás, politikai vagy más vélemény, nemzeti vagy társadalmi származás, vagyoni, születési vagy egyéb helyzet szerinti különbségtétel nélkül.

(2) Az embereknek az (1) bekezdés szerinti bármilyen hátrányos megkülönböztetését a törvény szigorúan bünteti. . . .

54. § (1) In the Republic of Hungary everyone shall have the inherent right to life and human dignity; no one shall be deprived of these rights. . . .

61. § (1) In the Republic of Hungary everyone shall have the right to freedom of expression and to freedom of speech, and furthermore to the right to receive and impart information of public interest. . . .

70/A. § (1) The Republic of Hungary shall ensure the human rights and civil rights for all persons on her territory without any kind of discrimination, such as on the basis of race, color, gender, language, religion, political or other opinion, national or social origin, financial situation, birth, or on any other grounds whatsoever.

(2) Any kind of discrimination described in subsection (1) shall be strictly penalized by statute. . . .[13]

The dilemma is clearly present in the language of the Constitution. The above excerpts show that the Constitution considers "human dignity" an "inherent right" and considers the "freedom of expression" another "right." It also proposes that "discrimination" ought to be "penalized" because it violates "human rights and civil rights for all persons."

Let us look at two excerpts taken from the committee sittings and investigate the patterned use of the key symbol "violation of human dignity" in relation to two other symbols, "hate speech" and "Constitution." The first excerpt is from the bill proposed by the Hungarian government, Bill No. T/5179.[14] A copy of the bill was available to all participants of the nine committee sittings. We can view the text as a concise formulation of what MPs in favor of the criminal punishment of hate speech argued at the committee meetings.

Excerpt 4.2

A véleménynyilvánítás szabadsága és a szólásszabadság a demokratikus társadalom, a közösségi együttélés alapvető eleme, ugyanakkor e jogok tartalma nem jelentheti azt, hogy e jogokkal visszaélve a szabadságjogokat bárki csorbíthatja. . . .

A Javaslat szerinti (2) bekezdés a Btk. 269. §-ának keretein belül biztosítja azon elkövető megbüntetését, aki nagy nyilvánosság előtt az emberi méltóságot azáltal sérti, hogy mást vagy másokat a nemzeti, etnikai, faji, vagy vallási hovatartozás miatt becsmérel vagy megaláz [(2) bekezdés a) pont], illetőleg aki azt állítja, hogy a nemzeti, etnikai, faji vagy vallási hovatartozás alapján valamely személy vagy a személyek egy csoportja alsóbb- vagy felsőbbrendű [(2) bekezdés b) pont].

A Javaslat szerint tehát az emberi méltóságnak a (2) bekezdés a) és b) pontja szerinti megsértése csak akkor büntetendő, ha azt nagy nyilvánosság előtt követik el.

A "nagy nyilvánosság előtti elkövetés," illetve az "emberi méltóság megsértése" olyan objektív, külső korlátok, amelyekből adódóan a véleménynyilvánítás szabadságának—mint kiemelt alkotmányjogi védelmet élvező kommunikációs anyajognak—a büntetőjogi eszközökkel történő korlátozása alkotmányos keretek között maradhat.

Nem hagyható figyelmen kívül továbbá az sem, hogy a véleménynyilvánítás szabadsága általában mindenféle közlés szabadságát magában foglalja, függetlenül a közlés módjától és értékétől, és többnyire annak valóságtartalmától is. . . .

E mellett a büntetőjogi felelősséghez szükséges "az emberi méltóság megsértése" is, amelynek indoka, hogy az elkövető ezzel elvitatja a mindenkit megillető egyenlőség jogát, azt, hogy az alkotmányos jogok teljességét élvezze a támadott csoport vagy személy.

Az emberi méltósághoz való jog alkotmányos alapjog, ezáltal pedig a véleményszabadsággal konkuráló érték, tehát ennek külső korlátja lehet, különösen azért, mert a köznyugalom megzavarása nagyszámú egyéni jog megsértésének veszélyével fenyeget.

The freedom of opinion and the freedom of expression are fundamental elements of democratic society and communal life. However, the contents of these rights cannot be taken to mean that anyone may curtail the franchise of others by abusing these rights. . . .

Within the framework of article 269 of the criminal code, section (2) of the bill guarantees the punishment of a perpetrator who in front of the public at large violates human dignity by defaming or humiliating another person or persons on the basis of their national, ethnic, racial, or religious membership [section (2) item a)], or who declares that on the basis of their national, ethnic, racial, or religious membership a certain person or group of persons is inferior or superior [section (2) item b)]. Therefore, according to the bill a violation against human dignity according to items a) and b) of section 2 must be punished only if it is perpetrated in front of the public at large.

"Perpetration in front of the public at large" and "violation of human dignity" are objective, external limits that imply that the limitations imposed on the freedom of opinion (as a fundamental communicative right enjoying heightened constitutional protection) by means included in the criminal code will not exceed the limits of the constitutional framework. It should be noted that the freedom of opinion usually entails the freedom of all kinds of statements regardless of the manner, quality, and most often the truth content of the statement. . . .

In addition, the "violation of human dignity" is also necessary for the establishment of criminal responsibility. The justification for this is that by means of this violation the perpetrator contests the right of equality that behooves everyone, in other words, the attacked group's or individual's right to enjoy the fullness of constitutional rights.

The right to human dignity is a fundamental constitutional right, and, as such, a value concurrent with the freedom of opinion. Therefore, it can serve as the external limit of the freedom of opinion, specifically since the disturbance of public peace threatens with the violation of a large number of individual rights.

Let us map out the relationships among key symbols in this somewhat lengthy excerpt in order to develop an understanding of their meanings. The above excerpt places the symbol "violation of human dignity" with the key symbols of "freedom of opinion" and "Constitution" in relationships of co-occurrence (i.e., in relationships where they are neither synonyms nor antonyms, but are semantically related). "Freedom of opinion" stands in a relationship of substitutability with "freedom of expression"—that is, the two can stand in for each other. Obviously, this is not to say that there are no other key symbols associated with "violation of human dignity"; I am highlighting these symbols to point to a communicative pattern. The document suggests the following rule for the interpretation of the violation of human dignity: When a person in front of the public at large defames or humiliates another person or persons on the basis of their national, ethnic, racial, or religious membership, or declares that on the basis of their national, ethnic, racial, or religious membership a certain person or group of persons is inferior or superior—and, by implication, when that person contests the right of the attacked group or individual to enjoy the fullness of constitutional rights—that person counts as a violator of human dignity.

In excerpt 4.2, the relationship of co-occurrence between the "violation of human dignity" and "hate speech" symbols is implicit even though the actual term "hate speech" is not mentioned in the document. It is taken-for-granted knowledge at these sittings that the central concern of the bill is hate speech. As a mode of "abusing these rights," *gyűlöletbeszéd* is also in a relationship of contrast with the freedom of opinion. This relationship among the key symbols can be summed up in the following cultural proposition: hate speech is a violation of human dignity and is therefore to be seen as a mode of speaking not protected by the Constitution, which protects only expression that does not violate human dignity.

In the third excerpt, MP Dr. Gábor Fodor is speaking on behalf of his political party (the Alliance of Free Democrats, or SZDSZ, the largest left-wing Hungarian liberal party), explaining the party's official stance toward the proposed bill. The excerpt was taken from the transcript of a Committee on Human Rights, Minorities, Civil, and Religious Affairs sitting.

Excerpt 4.3

Elöljáróban szeretném leszögezni, a Szabad Demokraták Szövetségének az az álláspontja—és a hagyományai is arra kötelezik -, hogy a leghatározottabban fel kell lépni a gyűlöletbeszéd és minden olyan magatartás ellen, amely embereket sérthet emberi méltóságukban kisebbséghez való tartozásuk, illetve bármilyen véleményük vagy álláspontjuk miatt. Ez a fellépés kívánatos, sőt véleményünk szerint nem volt elegendő az a fellépés, ami idáig Magyarországon történt. Az előttünk fekvő törvényjavaslatról viszont az a véleményünk, alkalmatlan arra, hogy ebben az ügyben segítséget nyújtson és szolgálja azt a fellépési kívánalmat, amit az előbb megfogalmaztam.

Azért alkalmatlan erre ez a javaslat, mert itt a véleménynyilvánítás olyan típusú korlátozásáról van szó, ami az előbb hivatkozott alkotmánybírósági döntés és a legfelsőbb bírósági állásfoglalások fényében nem megengedhető. . . .

Egyébiránt pedig jelen pillanatban is fel lehet lépni Magyarországon a gyűlöletbeszéd és minden olyan típusú magatartás ellen, ami a kisebbségek ellen vagy—még egyszer hangsúlyozom—bármiféle emberi méltóság megsértésére irányul. Ehhez a jogi eszközök rendelkezésre állnak. . . .

Az pedig—azt gondolom—nekünk ebben a bizottságban, nekünk megint csak különösen kötelezettségünk, hogy az alapvető véleménynyilvánítás és a gondolat szabadságát semmilyen körülmények között ne engedjük korlátozni, még oly nemesnek tetsző célok érdekében sem.

By way of an introduction I would like to assert that the standpoint of the Alliance of Free Democrats—in accordance with the party's traditions—is that hate speech must be firmly sanctioned along with all types of conduct that can violate human dignity based on the person's membership in a minority, or their opinion or standpoint. Such sanctioning is desirable, and, I will add, prosecution in Hungary so far hasn't been sufficient in our opinion. Regarding the bill in front of us, our opinion is that it is an inadequate way of providing help related to this issue and of serving the need for sanctioning that I have previously addressed.

The bill is insufficient because it involves restricting the right to free expression in such a way that is not permissible in the light of the previously referenced decision of the Constitutional Court and of a number of Supreme Court rulings. . . .

In addition, the sanctioning of hate speech and all acts directed against minorities or, I will emphasize again, of acts intended to violate any kind of human dignity is currently possible in Hungary. The legal provisions are available. . . .

And I think that for us in this committee, it is our specific obligation not to allow the curtailing of the freedom of opinion and thought under any circumstances, not even in the name of seemingly noble causes.[15]

In this excerpt, the relationship of co-occurrence between the key symbols is clear: *gyűlöletbeszéd* is an act that violates human dignity. But the relationship between hate speech and free expression/freedom of opinion is more complicated. (Free expression and freedom of opinion are, once again, in a relationship of substitutability.) It appears that Fodor is drawing a distinction between legally sanctionable hate speech and free expression that the proposed law would render legally sanctionable *as* hate speech, despite of the high courts' recent decisions. This subtle distinction is grounded in the ambiguous use of the term *fellépés* (sanctioning). In this linguistic context, sanctioning can mean two things: implementing legal sanctions or publicly taking a stand against hate speech. Fodor is arguing against an expanded interpretation of hate speech that, he proposes, the bill under consideration is trying to advocate while carefully avoiding the impression that he is protecting hate speech in general. The danger inherent in the unconstitutional move of expanding the legal meaning of hate speech, Fodor implies, is that the bill would place some free speech into a relationship of co-occurrence with hate speech.[16] As a result, one fundamental human right (freedom of speech) would be compromised for the sake of another (human dignity). The relationship between what the bill identifies as hate speech and the two mutually substitutable symbols (freedom of opinion/freedom of speech) is that of co-occurrence: this type of hate speech constitutes a type of free expression. Thus we arrive at the following cultural proposition: hate speech that the

Constitutional Court did not define as a criminal act is a mode of free expression and, as such, is protected by the Constitution, even though such hate speech can violate others' constitutional right to human dignity.

The two cultural propositions stated above stand in obvious contrast. Each can be reformulated in a way that explicitly links symbols and symbolic relations only implicitly present in both excerpts.

> 1. Hate speech violates the human dignity of others. Human dignity is protected by the Constitution. The freedom of expression is also protected by the Constitution. Since the right to human dignity and the right to free expression are both within the Constitution, one can serve as the limit to the other. Therefore, hate speech is a mode of expression not protected by the Constitution.

> 2. Hate speech violates the human dignity of others. Human dignity is protected by the Constitution. The freedom of expression is also protected by the Constitution. Since the right to human dignity and the right to free expression are both within the Constitution, one cannot be compromised for the sake of the other. Therefore, hate speech is a mode of expression protected by the Constitution.

The bill and the speaker reach contrasting conclusions based on the same legal premises. I suggest that this contrast can be explained by identifying two mediating terms (higher-order symbolic terms that organize lower-order symbol systems) in the excerpts. In excerpt 4.2, the text of the bill makes a reference to the freedom of opinion and the freedom of expression as fundamental elements of "communal life." If "community" serves as the basis of the interpretation of the relationship between the Constitution and expressive behavior, then the expressive conduct of one member of the community that violates the dignity of another member of the community will be interpreted as unconstitutional. Because every citizen is a member of the same (national, Hungarian) community, a community partially created and sustained by the Constitution, the freedom of one member will stretch only as far as the freedom of the other.

The argument of the speaker in excerpt 4.3 is organized by a different mediating term, the "individual." Considering that the speaker is speaking as a representative of the Hungarian Liberal party, SZDSZ, we can safely say that his presentation relies on the individual as a key element of the party's political rhetoric. This is reflected in SZDSZ's 1988 Declaration of Principles, which was later adopted as the articulation of the party's basic principles: "Our rights are rooted in our human nature, we do not receive them as a reward for serving the interest of the 'community' in proportion to the amount of service we perform. . . . We are fighting for the political rights of the individual" (Jogaink ember mivoltunkban gyökereznek, s nem a "közösség" javára végzett szolgálat jutalmaként nyerjük el őket a szolgálat arányában. . . . Harcolunk az egyén politikai jogaiért).[17] If we accept that the Hungarian Constitution is first and foremost a collection of the individual's fundamental rights, then we must also accept that the individual's freedom of expression cannot be limited, from the perspective of constitutionality, on the basis of the violation of the human dignity of another. The individual's human dignity is violated if a restriction is imposed on the freedom of expression, which is an outcome that, from this vantage point, is unconstitutional.

We have arrived at a point of the analysis where cultural beliefs about the nature of persons can be formulated. Excerpt 4.2 implies a model of personhood in which the person is to be seen primarily as *a member of a national community*. Excerpt 4.3 implies a model of personhood in which the person is to be regarded, first and foremost, as *an individual (separate from a community)*. These communal and individualistic models of personhood explain the two opposing interpretations of the Constitution of Hungary. One interpretation suggests that the Constitution protects the rights of persons as members of a community, whereas the other implies that the Constitution protects the rights of persons as individuals.

What about appropriate sanctions against *gyűlöletbeszéd*? We have seen that there is agreement among MPs that hate speech calls for action. But the norms they derive from conflicting interpretations of the Constitution are also at odds. The norm that goes with the community-based interpretation of the Constitution is a proscription, the other is a prescription:

Proscription: In the context of the public sphere, if one wants to act against hate speech, one ought not constrain the freedom of expression by law.

Prescription: In the context of the public sphere, if one wants to act against hate speech, one ought constrain the freedom of expression by law.

These norms, in turn, shape participants' conceptions of appropriate action in the public sphere against hate speech. Those committee members who defended the bill (from the Hungarian Socialist Party) suggested that the most appropriate action to be taken against hate speech is passing the bill into law. Those who opposed the bill (all other committee members) suggested the more rigorous implementation of existing laws within the penal code, increased willingness on the part of the judiciary and the police to implement existing laws, and the elite's commitment to providing a good example to the public as appropriate sanctions against hate speech. The elite includes the judiciary, who could set a good example by prosecuting hate speech–related crimes based on existing laws, and other public actors, such as politicians or media personalities, who have access to public forums for making public statements condemning hate speech.[18]

Cultural Norms

Before going any further, it is important to clarify what I mean by norms. Following Brad Hall, we can distinguish three traditions in social scientific research on norms.[19] The normative force (or Parsonian) position on norms holds them to be, in essence, the social DNA of a community. People in societies internalize social norms in the process of socialization. Social norms are enforced through sanctions. As a result of sanctions and socialization, norms acquire an almost deterministic power over people's actions and make the prediction of action possible. The second, interpretive position denies the causal link between actions and norms. The relationship between the two, this position suggests, is negotiated in each and every communicative situation. People invoke norms to account for social order, but norms don't constitute that order. Instead, they are best thought of as one cultural resource people can rely on to make sense of complicated and problematic situations. Norms do not guide action, interpretivists argue—rather, it is the meanings that participants negotiate and assign to actions in the moment of interaction that are key.

The third position on norms, the one Hall refers to as the discursive position, holds that the other two are misguided. People are not robots running the software of social norms, as the normative force position suggests. The argument that the knowledge of norms predicts one's actions is somewhat naïve. But the opposite picture of norms, the one that the interpretive position advocates, is also inaccurate. Norms are not entirely fluid, and their force applies across communicative situations. The discursive force position establishes a middle ground between the normative force and interpretivist positions by suggesting that norms are indeed a resource that people can use to interpret and evaluate their own and others' actions, but that they also constrain action. Norms allow communicators to produce social action that is in line with their community's sense of appropriate and acceptable conduct, and they also allow them to identify social action that violates communal morality. By implication, norms also allow people to act in ways that their communities find objectionable. It all depends on what a social actor wants to accomplish in a given interactional moment. Because norms exist in communicative practice, and communicative practice is necessarily tied to culture, norms are best thought of as culturally variable.

Let us take the proscription against legal sanctions ("one ought not constrain the freedom of expression by law") as an example to briefly demonstrate the difference among the three approaches to norms. According to the normative force position, when MP Gábor Fodor says, "It is our specific obligation not to allow the curtailing of the freedom of opinion and thought under any circumstances, not even in the name of seemingly noble causes," he simply names the norm to whose force he is yielding. The interpretive position would say that here Fodor invokes a norm (the obligation) in order to creatively shape how his fellow MPs make sense of hate speech and the possibility of legal sanctioning, and more generally, how the discussion during the meeting will unfold. The discursive position, the approach to norms I use here, notes two things about Fodor's utterance. First, Fodor invokes a norm here because he is responding to a norm violation, the suggestion that hate speech that does not pose clear and present danger to the target should be made the subject of criminal sanctions. Second, he does so because he wants to present himself as the protector of his community's moral order, the order we may call "democracy." In a democracy, Fodor argues, the unnecessary criminalization of speech is a serious violation of the human right to free expression. Therefore, the suggestion to criminalize speech violates the norms of the community and, at the same time, places those who advocate criminal sanctions outside the moral order of democracy.

From a discourse perspective, Fodor taps into a cultural norm made available to him by his community in order to undermine his political opponents' position and credibility through moral one-upmanship. The community offering him this norm is actually not one but two overlapping communities. He is speaking as a member of a political group organized around liberal notions of society. The norm he is invoking derives from that ideology. In addition, he is speaking as a Hungarian politician displaying concern for his entire nation. The other community that functions as the source of the norm is thus the Hungarian nation, the political system that accepts liberal ideology as a legitimate way of thinking about society. This is of course not to say that all Hungarians are liberals. What I mean is that the Hungarian speech community acknowledges that the liberal take on free expression exists, it is coherent, and there are people who think of it as their own.

Norms are a powerful means of constructing boundaries around groups of people and creating alignments between individuals and groups. Groups also use norms to align themselves with other groups. In the committee meetings

I discuss in this chapter, some MPs had to rely on norms for boundary work because of a curious political situation: conservatives found themselves united with liberals against the proposal to criminalize hate speech. In a country where the left and the right tend to think of themselves as parallel universes, a party on the left (the Alliance of Free Democrats, SZDSZ) became discursively and politically aligned with two parties on the center–right (Fidesz and the Hungarian Democratic Forum, MDF) against the liberals' coalition partner (the Hungarian Socialist Party, MSZP). Concerned about the political advantage the left would gain as a result of the passage of the hate speech bill, Fidesz and MDF were suddenly forced to play a double game: they had to defeat the bill with the liberals and they had to avoid being confused with the liberals. Consider the following statement by a Fidesz MP, Róbert Répássy: "There are those who respect the Constitution—we don't belong among the liberals, nor among the racists, we belong among those who respect the Constitution and therefore we do not support the bill."[20] In this brief excerpt, the speaker accomplishes a delicate balancing act by means of invoking a cultural norm. He explicitly distances himself from the "liberals" while basing Fidesz's decision to oppose the bill on the party's "respect [for] the Constitution." Hence he is able to cast the temporary political alliance with the liberals as one not between parties but between groups of citizens concerned about constitutional rights. In addition, by distancing his party from "racists" he is careful to dismiss a frequently heard allegation from the left that Fidesz's lack of support for the hate speech bill stems from the party's desire to court Hungarian extreme right-wing voters.

The Cultural Foundations of Lawmaking and Deliberation

The majority of field-based work on hate speech and free expression proposes new ways of (or reasons for) molding existing legal procedures to communal moral systems, or changing those moral systems to accommodate universal legal principles. This was not my goal in this chapter; nor was it my goal to describe an exotic legal system with a quaint mechanism for settling disputes in society. Hungarian reasons for maintaining or curtailing complete freedom of expression probably sound familiar to most Western readers. The point of this chapter was to illustrate that in the Hungarian (or any other) cultural scene, lawmaking and deliberation are intricately tied to cultural conceptions of what it means to be a person, a citizen, and a politician, and what it means to sanction morally objectionable conduct. Lawmakers routinely use these meanings to achieve particular communicative ends. More precisely, they use them to create legal procedures in line with their respective worldviews and the moral and political agendas animating those worldviews.

In *Moral Politics*, the linguist George Lakoff argues that understanding the worldview behind political agendas is an essential criterion of successful party politics. Lamenting the political impotence of U.S. liberals during the George W. Bush presidency, Lakoff says that the "lack of conscious awareness of their own political worldview has been devastating to the liberal cause."[21] I would expand this argument and claim that creative political action takes into account key symbols related to a political issue in the political discourse of the day, the competing interpretations of those symbols, and the competing moralities that give meaning to those interpretations. As we have seen in this chapter, cultural thinking about symbols, meanings, and moralities can be used not only to address one's supporters and opponents but also to build and manage important political alliances.

Although the participants of the parliamentary debates endorsed competing interpretations of sanctions against hate speech on the basis of competing moralities, they agreed on one thing: hate speech is a mode of public expression that should be eradicated. In the following chapter I show that some social actors on the stage of Hungarian public discourse not only refused to accept this moral common denominator, they had also developed a variety of culturally based rhetorical strategies to undermine its coherence and credibility.

5

RHETORICAL RESISTANCE

During the height of the *gyűlöletbeszéd* debate, it was not uncommon in Hungarian political discourse to hear statements like these:

> The term "hate speech" is the Orwellian fabrication of the political left.

> People charge their opponents in public debate with hate speech just to shut them up.

> When they say we are guilty of hate speech, they only reveal that they are filled with hatred toward us. They are the ones speaking hate speech, not us!

In Hungary, hate speech is generally discussed as a type of derogatory public expression targeting ethnic minorities, such as Romanies (Gypsies) or Jews. Typically, when public figures propose that hate speech ought to be eradicated, they have racist hate speech in mind. The antiracist efforts of such public figures are robust and culturally coherent, but so is the rhetoric of those who question the legitimacy of their efforts. These critics, who deny the status of hate speech as a social issue, do not belong to a unified social or political movement. They are also a clear minority compared to the group of public figures who accept hate speech as a form of public expression about which Hungarians ought to be concerned. Their talk about hate speech, however, points to a set of cultural beliefs that an increasing number of Hungarians see as a powerful alternative to more mainstream beliefs about fundamental human rights.

Since the mid-1990s, Hungarian antiracist activists have been raising awareness about racist hate speech as a social issue and an evil plaguing contemporary Hungarian society. In chapter 3 I characterized this interpretation of hate speech as a form of verbal hygiene. This chapter is also concerned with verbal hygiene, but of a different kind. Here, the object of hygiene is not public expression defined and evaluated as "hate speech," but the term itself and the covert, insidious political agenda it is thought to label. This type of talk aims to transform the original issue (racist hate speech) into another issue (the hate speech agenda). I use the term "hate speech agenda" to refer collectively to three communicative forms: antiracist allegations of hate speech, the public circulation of the antiracist interpretation of hate speech, and various legislative proposals designed to turn hate speech into a criminal or civic offense. This chapter is concerned both with the kinds of arguments used against the antiracist use of the term *gyűlöletbeszéd* in Hungarian public discourse, and with how these arguments undermine the meaning of the term itself and the credibility of antiracist activism.

In recent years, rhetoric scholars have started to look beyond texts (e.g., speeches) into the realm of everyday language use. Reviewing a wide variety of theoretical perspectives on rhetoric, Hauser wrote, "Their differences notwithstanding, these perspectives share some basic premises about rhetoric as a mode of discourse and as a social practice. They agree that rhetoric is occasioned discourse; that it is addressed to an audience; that it is practical discourse concerned with issues of the day as they intersect with the concerns of the audience; that it is a mode of thinking suited to inducing and coordinating social action on contingent problems."[1]

Cultural thinking about public communication suggests that all action, including rhetorical action responding to contingent problems, takes place in a specific sociocultural context. In any community of speakers, rhetorical action builds on locally available cultural resources and their local meanings.[2] For example, one challenge for public speakers is that they must try to voice their opinions in ways that their audiences find plausible.[3] Plausibility can be achieved by meeting two criteria in the design of public expression, cohering and communing: the act of persuasion must constitute locally meaningful communicative conduct, and communal members must evaluate it as appropriate conduct.[4]

To someone who endorses and values universal human rights, anti-antiracist rhetoric may sound somewhat alien, even outlandish. Nevertheless, those who cast doubt on the hate speech agenda make sense to their audiences, and cultural analysis can uncover the logic of their rhetoric. I pursued that logic by analyzing the text of ten semi-structured, face-to-face interviews with Hungarian public figures in addition to the further analysis of the articles and broadcasts I discussed in earlier chapters. My interviews brought me into personal contact with some of the most notorious figures of the Hungarian radical right. I fervently disagreed with many things these speakers had said in public. However, in my pursuit of the ethnographic ideal of holistic cultural representation,[5] I felt it necessary to recruit them as interviewees and to fully appreciate the complexity of their perspectives on hate speech. One important trick in the ethnographer's toolbox is the ability to appreciate a perspective's complexity and coherence without necessarily appreciating or adopting the perspective itself.

While the cultural discourse approach can show the cultural foundations of plausibility or common sense in argument, the discourse approach is well suited to capture how speakers strategically appeal to elements of that common sense in argumentative discourse. These two approaches are complementary. Therefore, I draw on discourse analytic work on racism and antiracism[6] in explaining how speakers and writers use a variety of linguistic strategies and related semantic moves to present their positions as plausible in contrast with an opposing position. Following cultural discourse analytic methodology, I also identify and link key symbolic terms in order to understand how anti-antiracist speakers' rhetorical strategy is anchored in basic cultural beliefs (premises) about communally intelligible and appropriate models of who persons are (personhood) and how they should relate to one another in society (sociation).[7]

Argument and Rhetorical Strategy

In what follows I present excerpts from my materials that illustrate four key argumentative themes in the rhetoric of anti-antiracism: (1) the hate speech agenda is founded on the deliberate corruption of the Hungarian language; (2) the hate speech agenda reveals that antiracists are pursuing an alien political utopia; (3) the hate speech agenda is fraught with ideological inconsistency; and (4) antiracist proponents of the hate speech agenda are themselves filled with hatred. I outline the rhetorical strategies used to promote each of these themes and the cultural foundations of those strategies.

The Hate Speech Agenda Is Founded on the Deliberate Corruption of the Hungarian Language

The first excerpt comes from a newspaper article written by the influential Hungarian historian Mária Schmidt attacking the concept of hate speech. In the excerpt below, Schmidt begins with an account of the rise of "hatred" as a politically charged concept in Hungarian political discourse. She identifies the antiracist "Act against hatred!" movement in 1992 as the chief source of the widespread public use of the term.

Excerpt 5.1

A jelszó tetszetős. Érzékelteti, hogy a gyűlölet szégyenletes, ellene tenni pedig ildomos. A gyűlölet szó átpolitizálása és kompromittálása után Csepeli György a *Népszabadság* hasábjain diszkreditálta nyelvünk beszéddé összeálló szavait is: "a szó egyúttal cselekvés is . . . pusztán a szavak kimondása is sértés, tehát cselekvés. . . . Nem kell tehát valakit lelőnöm, vagy megpofoznom, ugyanezt szavakkal is megtehetem." Így érkeztünk el az új nyelvpolitikai leleményhez, a "gyűlöletbeszédhez." Azért kell tehát a törvény szigorával eljárni a gyűlöletbeszéddel szemben, mert a gyűlölet, mint olyan ellen úgy is tenni kell, a beszéd pedig eddigi felfogásunkkal szemben, ha gyűlölettel párosul, egyben cselekedet is. A tettekért pedig egy jogállamban felelni kell. Így tehát a jogállami normák nem sérülnek, ha a büntetőjog hatálya a szólásra is kiterjed. A "gyűlöletbeszéd" olyan értelmetlen és egyben definiálatlan szókapcsolat, melynek jelentése talán csak az osztályellenség vagy a nép ellensége fogalmakhoz hasonlítható, képzése pedig egyenesen orwelli.

The slogan ["Act against hatred!"] is an attractive one. It makes one feel that hatred is shameful and acting against it is commendable. Following the politicization and compromising of the word "hatred," György Csepeli also discredited the way words constitute speech in our language in an article in *Népszabadság*: "Words are also action . . . the utterance of words by itself constitutes action. . . . Hence I don't have to shoot or slap someone, I can do the same with words." This is how we arrive at the new invention in the politics of language, "hate speech." The reason why hate speech must be sanctioned with severe laws is that hatred as such must be acted against and speech, contrary to our existing conception of it, becomes action when combined with hatred. In a constitutional state, one must be held accountable for one's actions. Thus the norms of the constitutional state remain unbroken if we extend criminal law to speech. "Hate speech" is an unintelligible and undefined compound whose meaning can perhaps only be compared to concepts like class enemy or enemy of the people, and its construction is downright Orwellian.[8]

In chapter 1, the historical overview of the career of *gyűlöletbeszéd* and related terms gave us a sense of why some Hungarians felt a deep-seated suspicion toward antiracist allegations of hate speech. "Incitement," the equivalent of "hate speech" in legal discourse, was used frequently in communist Hungary to persecute antiestablishment artists and intellectuals. The hate speech agenda and its various proposals to limit freedom of expression disturbed those who, like Schmidt, were silenced by the communist regime.

Schmidt discusses hate speech as the product of politically motivated neologizing. As a result, she argues, the meanings of the words "hatred" and "speech," elements of "our language," are hopelessly lost. The word "hatred" became politicized and compromised in superficially "attractive" antiracist sloganeering. The commonsense idea of "speech" as a string of words was also "discredited." Schmidt suggests that Csepeli's coinage robs the word "speech" (*beszéd*) of its original meaning (words linked together to form speech) because, "contrary to our existing conception of [speech]," this "new invention in the politics of language" suggests that speech "becomes action when combined with hatred."

As "unintelligible and undefined" as hate speech may be, its appearance in public talk prepares the way for the criminalization of speech. For Schmidt, this manipulation of language in the service of the exercise of power is an unmistakably Orwellian move that brings to mind vacuous political terminology created and used for the persecution of citizens during communist times (such as "class enemy" and "enemy of the people"). "When words lose their meaning," Schmidt warns her readers, quoting Confucius, "people lose their freedom" (Amikor a szavak elvesztik jelentésüket, az emberek elvesztik szabadságukat).

Whose interests does this manipulation serve? At a later point in her article, Schmidt concludes that those who debate the necessity of legal sanctions against hate speech, pro and contra, are members of a small, militant, leftist intellectual elite who, following the fall of communism, are in dire need of a cause that would help them close their ranks. This new cause is the fight against hate speech or "Nazi speech," which, Schmidt argues, is essentially a fight against anti-Semitism. By keeping hate speech on the political agenda, these intellectuals aim to secure their position as opinion leaders on a Hungarian political scene dominated by a socialist–liberal government,[9] despite the fact that Hungarian Jews "did not ask for, and most likely do not require" protection against an "acute Nazi threat."[10]

Schmidt's words are rhetorically powerful because they present her as someone confronting and unmasking political evil. She adopts a critical stance toward an alleged linguistic maneuver by a leftist political movement, one that, to her mind, supports the left-wing government's attempt to repeat, or to continue, the communists' struggle for absolute authoritarian power. Schmidt joins the battle against the political foe by exercising verbal hygiene, by flagging the harmful manipulation of the Hungarian language. She treats political talk that defies linguistic common sense as evidence of political games that fundamentally undermine a nation's interests.

Schmidt's argument that hate speech is a corrupt and meaningless linguistic form serving an authoritarian political agenda is what discourse analysts would call an extended reversal move. Here, this move implies that antiracists' claim to higher moral authority by exposing hatred and hate speech in Hungarian society can be seen as evidence of their inferior moral standing. The reversal rests on an "us versus them" contrast. Further, Schmidt's argumentation conveniently conceals the fact that Hungarian antiracists do not stand united with regard to the legal sanctioning of hate speech.[11] This generalization move creates a united adversary whose moral standing is in contrast with "ours." Last, the author also presents herself as an expert of the antiracist view of hate speech. She accomplishes this by citing a concrete example and by slipping into the voice of the adversary. She, however, is careful not to let the display of expertise create the impression that she is taking the adversary's side. She maintains an accusatory frame by reminding the reader from time to time that she values the views she is representing negatively. Having established her expertise, she moves to expose the insidious character of the hate speech agenda.

The Hate Speech Agenda Reveals that Antiracists Are Pursuing an Alien Political Utopia

Some critics of Hungarian antiracist advocacy discuss hate speech as a rhetorical device designed to silence those who speak the truth about Hungarian social reality, and to dismiss speaking the truth as evidence of "hateful passions" (*gyűlöletteli indulat*).[12] The term *gyűlöletbeszéd*, in this view, is used to construct an artificial reality that denies actually existing social relations. When asked for his opinion about the antiracist use of hate speech in Hungary, one of my respondents, a former leader in the youth organization of Fidesz called Fidelitas, explained to me that antiracists are attempting to install a "*Star Trek* reality" in Hungary. This version of reality had very little to do with how individuals and ethnic groups living in and around Hungary related to one another. Those who advocate *Star Trek* reality will label as "hate speech" any kind of talk that undermines their vision.

Excerpt 5.2

INTERVIEWEE: Én úgy látom hogy ez[13] a mákony ez a dopping ez most egy ilyen újrateremtjük a világot az interneten meg a globalizáción keresztül és az a fasza gyerek aki globalizált cégnél fasza gyerek, az az ideáltípus, és aki meg mondjuk nem annyira szeretné ezt az meg az meg megrontja itt ezt a hú de színes világot. Amit itt most felépítünk. Ugye azért kérdeztem a CEU-t mert ott egy ilyen világtendencia van. Ugye hogy kell tehát így kötelező a csapatba bevenni a kínait mert kell a sorozatba a *Star Trekbe* kell a kínai arc, meg a *Star Trekbe* kell a néger csávó meg a *Star Trekbe* kell a leszbikus nő meg a (*inaudible*) vannak ezek a a csapat összeállítások.

[TURN OMITTED]

INTERVIEWEE: Ilyen amerikai munka, és ezek a fasza gyerekek, és a *Star Trek* megy előre és (*inaudible*). Aki meg így mondja hogy hát így kurvára nem ez a helyzet és a szerbek ölik a magyarokat meg viszont meg a bosnyákok a szerbeket meg a horvátok, s ezek tényleg egymás mellett élnek ötszáz éve, hát azért itt nem az a divat, hogy itt békében szeretjük egymást, az meg egy szarházi. Mert föllebbenti a fátylat.

INTERVIEWEE: The way I see it, now this opium or dope is this idea of let's re-create the world through the Internet and globalization, and the really cool people work at globalized corporations, they are the ideal types, and those who don't really want this are spoiling this oh-so-diverse world that we are busy building here. I mean, the reason why I asked you about CEU[14] is that what you see there is a world tendency. I mean that you have to, you are obliged to put a Chinese guy on the team, because you've got to have a Chinese guy in the series, you need the Chinese guy on *Star Trek*, and you need the black dude on *Star Trek*, and you need the lesbian woman on *Star Trek*, and you get these corporate team type of collectives.

[TURN OMITTED]

INTERVIEWEE: It's this American type of thing, and these are the cool people, and *Star Trek* forges ahead and [*inaudible*]. And people who say that this has nothing to do with the real situation and Serbs are killing Hungarians and vice versa, and Bosnians and Croats kill Serbs, and these folks have really lived side-by-side for five hundred years, loving each other in peace is not exactly fashionable here, people who say such things are considered jerks. Because they lift the veil.[15]

This speaker adopts a number of discursive elements from antiracist discourse. The Internet and globalization function in his talk as harbingers of a "fashionable" "oh-so-diverse world," where people of all nationalities, ethnicities, races, and sexual orientations (Chinese, black, lesbian) work together in "teams" inside "globalized corporations." An example of the same "world tendency" in the context of higher education is the Central European University in Budapest, where worldwide student recruitment is a matter of policy. My respondent introduces the analogy to *Star Trek*, the wildly popular U.S. sci-fi franchise. The analogy serves a dual purpose. On the one hand, the speaker uses it as a metaphor of diversity-based hiring policies ("you have to, you are obliged to put a Chinese guy on the team"). He is playfully suggesting that *Star Trek*, where characters include humans and various alien races, serves the model of the ideal corporate "team." On the other hand, references to *Star Trek* and to diversity point to global U.S. cultural influence. "It's this American type of thing," the speaker summarizes the vision of diversity, which he contrasts with a history of five hundred years of violence among ethnic groups in countries south of present-day Hungary. "Here" conjures up a central-eastern European reality, rooted deeply in local history and standing in stark contrast with the American, multinational, corporate, global-ized view of social relations.

This second theme directs our attention to hate speech as the locus of an ideo-logical struggle between proponents of diversity in the workplace and education, and those who point to the reality in central–eastern Europe, where "loving each other in peace is not exactly fashionable," and who attempt to "lift the veil" of utopia. We can see that the second theme builds on the "alien"/"local" dichot-omy, where the local is more real, and therefore of higher value, than the foreign. The reality of local social relations, my respondent suggests, is the product of an unbroken history that stretches over centuries. Alien ("American") social and moral orders (such as globalized and globalizing visions of diversity) that have no historical roots in the geopolitically defined locale that the speaker identifies as his own (central–eastern European) are of lower value and are less morally binding than the existing social order. Within this theme, diversity-based hiring or recruitment policies are also devalued on the grounds that they deny the social reality of the distinction between (ethnic, racial, sexual) majorities and minori-ties. Equal opportunity measures deny the social fact that the majority will be overrepresented in any social group. Combined with the alien/local dichotomy, this view turns this overrepresentation from fact into principle, according to which the "original" inhabitants of a given locale should have additional oppor-tunities over newcomers and minorities.

The alien/local dichotomy builds on and expands the "us versus them" con-trast strategy identified in the first section. It is not only that "we" (people who do not wish to deny central–eastern European social reality) stand in opposition to "them" (antiracists), but that "we" also represent and protect local "reality," whereas "they" are promoting an utopia of "diversity" that denies local social relations. Here, however, reversal happens on different grounds than in the first theme: "we" do not dispute antiracists' higher moral standing because it con-ceals an authoritarian political agenda, but because it is grounded in an alien sociopolitical ideology. The speaker makes direct appeals to common sense by referring to the "real situation" and those who "lift the veil." As does the speaker in excerpt 5.1, this speaker also uses the argumentative move of voicing the opponent's point of view to position himself as an expert of antiracist ideology and, by employing negative associations ("opium," "dope") and irony ("oh-so-diverse world"), to distance himself from that ideology. Ideological distancing is also marked by the frequent use of exaggeration ("let's re-create the world," "you are obliged to put the Chinese guy on the team," the murder of Hungarians and Serbs as an ongoing event). Finally, repetition lends additional weight to the speaker's argument that antiracist ideology is utopian (see the repeated references to *Star Trek*).

The Hate Speech Agenda Is Fraught with Ideological Inconsistency

Critics of the *gyűlöletbeszéd* agenda identify three types of inconsistency in antiracist advocacy. First, the argument goes, those who concurrently promote the concept of hate speech and freedom of expression run into a contradiction because they want to curtail free speech in order to prevent hate speech. Second, if those who promote hate speech are concerned about the well-being of minorities, they should also be concerned about violence against ethnic Hungarians (Magyars) living in neighboring countries. Third, if proponents of hate speech are concerned about discrimination they should stop discriminating against the majority society in Hungary by offering minorities additional protection from hate speech. To the critics, these inconsistencies are evidence that what motivates anti–hate speech advocacy can only be political interest, not genuine concern.

In excerpt 5.3, one of my respondents, the ideological leader of a small far-right group, responds to a general question about the meaning of the term "hate speech." He uses the first type of inconsistency argument and explicates the contradiction between the liberal doctrine of free expression and his group's argument for restricting free expression.

Excerpt 5.3

INTERVIEWEE: Tehát nyilvánvaló, hogy nem túl régi maga a fogalom. Meglehetősen politikai indítással keletkezett és angolszász talajon. És noha általánosnak látszik, mindenféle gyűlölet elítélése, nyilvánvaló, hogy olyan politikai indításból született, hogy korlátozza egyébként a liberalizmus által meghirdetett szólásszabadságot. Van aki szoktak hivatkozni a liberális Voltaire-re, hogy aki azt mondta hogy nem értek egyet veled semmiben. De az életemet áldoznám hogy elmond a véleményedet. Ez az elmélet. Nos ettől meglehetősen eltérő, sőt ezzel ellentétesnek látjuk azt az értelmezést azt az interpretációt amit a gyűlöletbeszédnek adnak napjainkban, ugyanis szólásszabadságnak, a liberalizmus által oltárra emelt szólásszabadságnak a korlátozását. A mi felfogásunk szerint nem korlátlanok a szabadságjogok, természetesen, hanem az erkölcsi rend egy hierarchikus egészt alkot, és természetesen a szólásszabadság más becsületére káros dolgokat nem hirdethet.

INTERVIEWEE: It is obvious that the concept [hate speech] is not an old one. It originated on Anglo-Saxon soil, from a definite political agenda. And although the condemnation of all hatred seems universal, it is obvious that the term was born from the political desire to restrict what is otherwise a key element of the liberal agenda: freedom of expression. Some refer to Voltaire, a liberal, who said I don't agree with you about anything. But I would sacrifice my life to have you speak your opinion. This is the theory. Now, we think that the sense made of the interpretation of hate speech today diverges from this theory, in fact we see this interpretation run counter to it. This interpretation is the restriction of freedom of speech, the freedom of speech glorified by liberals. In our view, human rights are not boundless, instead we observe a moral order forming a hierarchical whole, and of course free expression cannot teach things that violate another person's honor.[16]

The speaker links hate speech to a political agenda and to a foreign (Anglo-Saxon) origin. The political agenda, which the speaker implicitly—and, at a later point in the interview, explicitly—associates with "liberals," includes "restrict[ing] . . . freedom of expression." Although in the liberal use of the term "hate speech," "the condemnation of all hatred seems universal," this is only an appearance. The real purpose of the term is the restriction of certain types of speech of which liberals disapprove. Liberal morality fails to honor one of its own core principles, according to which "I don't agree with you about anything. But I would sacrifice my life to have you speak your opinion." This moral order, my respondent suggests, can and should be supplanted by one he calls "our view." In this "moral order forming a hierarchical whole," the right to free expression is of lower rank than "another person's honor" and can therefore be restricted without moral self-compromise.

This speaker also relies on the strategy of displaying expert understanding of the opponent's position in order to present himself as an authority on the subject of hate speech. The speaker's generalizing move, designed to portray a united adversary (i.e., liberals stand in for Hungarian antiracism), conceals a misrepresentation. In chapter 4 we saw that this is far from being the case: most Hungarian antiracist liberals tend to deny the value of anti–hate speech legislation.

An extended reversal strategy used in this excerpt consists of three different contrast moves, the second component of which sometimes remains implicit: "they" borrow alien, Anglo-Saxon words (whereas "we" rely on Hungarian words); "their" use of hate speech is motivated by "a definite political agenda" (whereas "we" have no such agenda); and "their" theory of free expression is at odds with practice, whereas our "moral order" forms a "whole" that is capable of curtailing free expression without logical contradictions on the grounds of the violation of another person's "honor." Taken together, these three contrast moves add up to an overall reversal strategy designed to drive the point home that although antiracists seek to occupy a higher moral plane than "ours," "our" moral system is superior to "theirs" because it can accomplish what "theirs" cannot: the intellectually and morally grounded limitation of free expression *and* the protection of honor.

These contrast moves, I would argue, are also designed to preempt the charge that the far right, including the group the speaker is speaking for, is immoral because, as a collective of speakers of hate speech, it has no respect for human rights. The speaker suggests that this is not the case. The far right is moral precisely *because* it recognizes that "human rights are not boundless" and curtails free expression to protect "honor." The speaker thus posits the existence of a particular type of morality, which functions independently of liberal moral order and deflects the anticipated charge of disrespect for human rights by locating human rights within this alternative morality.

Antiracist Proponents of the Hate Speech Agenda Are Themselves Filled with Hatred

The fourth theme captures the argument that antiracists are in fact more hateful than those they wish to prosecute in the name of the hate speech agenda. Excerpt 5.4 illustrates this theme. A caller to the televised call-in program *Kérdések órája Csintalan Sándorral* (An hour of questions with Sándor Csintalan) lists the names of Hungarian liberal and socialist politicians who, she says, regularly display a hateful demeanor. The caller takes issue with this because the proposed hate speech law is sponsored by the socialist–liberal parliamentary coalition.

Excerpt 5.4

CALLER: Azt szeretném tudni, hogy néznek-e tükörbe például Lendvai Ildikó, Eörsi Mátyás, Demszky Gábor, Szabó Zoltán? Ugyanis ezeknek a személyeknek sugárzik az arcáról a gyűlölet, amikor csak hallják Orbán Viktor nevét. És talán mindenki emlékszik még, ami néhány évvel ezelőtt történt, arra az esetre, amikor Orbánné Anikó asszony a negyedik gyermekének adott életet. Mit is mondott akkor a Szanyi Tibor? Már megint ellett az Orbánné.

CSINTALAN: Ja ja.

CALLER: Emlékszik rá?

CSINTALAN: Igen, emlékszem.

CALLER: Hát az mi volt, ha nem gyűlöletbeszéd?

CSINTALAN: Igen. Otromba bunkó.

CALLER: Na és Kovács László volt külügyminisztert sem felejtettük el, és az utódja, Hiller István arca is sötétbe borul, ha csak hallja is Orbán Viktor nevét. Tehát jó lenne azzal a gyűlöletbeszéd-törvénnyel egy kicsit vigyázni, ez igaz.

CALLER: I would like to know whether Ildikó Lendvai, Mátyás Eörsi, Gábor Demszky, Zoltán Szabó ever look at themselves in the mirror. Because the faces of these people radiate with hatred when they as much as hear Viktor Orbán's name. And perhaps everyone still remembers what happened a few years ago when Mrs. Orbán, Lady Anikó, gave birth to their fourth child. What did Tibor Szanyi say then? Mrs. Orbán pushed one out yet again.

CSINTALAN: Yeah, yeah.

CALLER: Do you remember?

CSINTALAN: Yes, I do.

CALLER: What was that if not hate speech?

CSINTALAN: Yes, what a jerk.

CALLER: And we haven't forgotten former foreign minister László Kovács either, and the face of his successor, István Hiller, also darkens when he hears [conservative prime minister] Viktor Orbán's name. So one should be a bit careful with that hate speech law, that's true.[17]

The caller and the host jointly support the caller's position, namely, that proponents of the antiracist *gyűlöletbeszéd* agenda themselves harbor irrational hatred. The caller points to two tokens of socialist–liberal hatred: "the faces of these people radiate with hatred when they as much as hear Viktor Orbán's name," and Tibor Szanyi's alleged utterance ("Mrs. Orbán pushed one out yet again"). The first token discredits the members of the coalition government because their reaction to an opposition politician is marked by the emotion of hatred. The second token discredits them because the hate speech of one of their members, by the force of synecdoche, casts them all as performers of hate speech. In a classic reversal move, the caller issues a warning to the governing left-wing coalition: they "should be a bit careful with that hate speech law," because they may end up prosecuting their own. This move partially rests on the host's and the caller's jointly produced interpretation of hate speech as the manifestation of the emotion of hatred in talk. This interpretation rids hate speech of its anti-racist meaning and moral charge, and expands its meaning to include *all* uncivil talk that serves as the vehicle of hatred. The caller and the host manage to use the tone-based interpretation of hate speech to squeeze the antiracist content-oriented interpretation out of consideration.

These two speakers leave implicit one implication of the reversal, namely, that the exposure of the opponent's lack of judgment places them on a higher moral plane. A rapid-fire presentation of contiguous examples of "hatred" on the Hungarian left bolsters this judgment. The caller presents a rhetorically overwhelming amount of evidence for the left's moral culpability. The barrage of examples is designed to ground the implicit moral charge in common sense by letting the *amount* of factual examples speak for itself. It is the weight of the evidence that is expected to have persuasive power here, instead of the simple statement of moral superiority.

Cultural and Rhetorical Foundations

The cultural analysis of these arguments and strategies reveals that, although a coherent anti-antiracist movement may not exist in Hungary, anti-antiracist talk is organized around a finite set of symbols and cultural premises. The type of talk analyzed in this chapter is informed by a system of symbolic linkages organized around the core symbols of "we"/"us" (as a locally conceived social order), ("our" vs. "their") "language," and (geographically, historically, socially, and morally defined) "place." These three core symbols stand in a relationship of mutual constitution. The "we" constitutes language as belonging either to "us" or to "others" (liberals, Anglo-Saxons, Orwellian oppressors) who live "here." "Language," and especially its spoken and written use, defines who "we" are, where "we" live, and what "we" believe to be a morally informed way of relating to others (e.g., speaking in ways that protects others' honor). "Place" is the locus of "our" reality (as opposed to American, corporate, or *Star Trek* faux realities) marked by historically shaped social and moral relations and "our" language. Finally, "place" and "language" not only give "us" our identity, they also derive their identity from the fact that "we" use the "language," and "we" inhabit the "place." This cultural model of social relations firmly anchors social relations among individual persons in the group defined by, and expressed in, a particular language used in a particular place. Moreover, it uses the group–language–place triad to evaluate the hate speech agenda as a violation of appropriate social relations.

To capture the rhetorical aspect of Hungarian anti-antiracist discourse, let us summarize the most significant rhetorical strategies employed to render arguments more plausible. First, speakers seek to achieve positive self-presentation by means of exposing the hidden political agenda and fallacies of the opponent. Second, they let the audience draw the conclusion that the opponent is morally inferior based on factual evidence. They also leave implicit the claim to their own higher moral standing. Third, they treat antiracists as a united political faction with a unified "hate speech" agenda. Fourth, they display expertise on the antiracist position on *gyűlöletbeszéd* without acknowledging the antiracist value and belief system informing that position. Finally, they avoid concession to the opponent's position even when displaying expertise on that position (e.g., by means of negative association, negative predication, irony). These strategies do not derive their rhetorical power from their accurate representation of social reality in some objective sense. They are powerful because they are founded on a view of social and political relations that provides the audience with a plausible and persuasive model of the relationship between good and evil in Hungarian public life.

I began this chapter by suggesting that anti-antiracist arguments are complex and robust. They possess these characteristics not because they are endorsed and advocated, in a wholesale manner, by particular social or political groups, but because they build on a particular cultural model of sociation and exhibit an identifiable set of rhetorical strategies. This model and these strategies mutually support one another. An example of the symbiotic relationship between the cultural and the rhetorical is the parallel use of the our versus alien (cultural) and the us versus them (rhetorical) dichotomies. In this vision of essential difference between an in-group and an out-group, a difference that separates and defines both groups, the rhetorical dichotomy brings the cultural one into play and the cultural renders the rhetorical meaningful.

The constitutive relationship among "our" group and the places or locales (nation, region) where "we" belong resonates with Gill Seidel's analysis of British anti-antiracist discourse.[18] Seidel characterizes the relationship between individual, groups, and nation imminent in that discourse as a "mystical notion of nationhood and national identity." The case of Hungarian anti-antiracist discourse extends this "mystical notion" to include regions and language besides group and nation. From this perspective, the hate speech agenda endangers the symbiotic relationship by disrupting the process of mutual constitution between group, language, and place. The disruption stems from two sources. First, the alien social ideal of "diversity" is seen to divorce persons from their groups and locales and mix them together into a "globalized" collective. Second, the very term "hate speech" is interpreted as an alien, "unintelligible and undefined" element in the Hungarian language, whose presence undermines "our" common-sense understanding of the separation between words and action. This second disruption jeopardizes the purity and coherence of language, a central expression of group and national identity.

Hygiene Without a Shared Sense of Health

All human communicative conduct can be viewed as cultural in the sense that audiences of communicative conduct make sense of and evaluate that conduct on the basis of variable systems of cultural codes (symbols, meanings, premises, and rules).[19] Knowledge of a given set of cultural codes is an important step toward learning to interact with a sociocultural group that relies on that set to live their everyday lives.[20] Cultural codes, like the rules of any game, enable and constrain human conduct and stake out a domain of meaning within which sensible, appropriate, and creative action is possible.[21] These theoretical statements are more likely to conjure up the image of someone trying to function socially in a foreign country than of someone debating a contentious social issue in public. It is, however, entirely possible that competing interpretations and responses to social issues are founded on competing cultural codes. Baxter calls those groups of people who use one set of codes instead of another within the same community of speakers "code communities."[22] Chapters 3, 4, and 5 of this book trace the outlines of two code communities that exist within the context of Hungarian public discourse. One community subscribes to this rule of interpretation: when talking about hate speech, use the term to refer to actual, observable acts of public expression that can be, and should be, labeled as *gyűlöletbeszéd*. The rule defining the other community can be phrased as follows: when talking about "hate speech," use the term to refer to the political agenda of your opponents.

Persistent social issues like racism force interested and invested social actors to reflect on their routine responses to the issue. Take the example of antiracist advocacy. Recently, prominent discourse analysts have begun to question the effectiveness of dominant modes of antiracist discourse. Essed[23] worries that modern antiracism often produces unproductive polarization by pitting antiracist "good guys" against racist "bad guys." Fairclough warns that antiracist talk is sometimes marked by "the arrogance, self-righteousness and puritanism of an ultra-left politics,"[24] a style that conservatives and moderate antiracists find equally unpalatable. The call to "say no to racism" has limited efficacy as a normative challenge because those who are charged with racism can simply respond by denying their own racism.[25]

Hungarian public discourse targeting racist hate speech not only produces polarizing talk and rhetorical resistance, but also illustrates the curiously reversible nature of antiracist talk. Antiracist discourse dedicated to exposing and sanctioning instances of public hate speech inevitably introduces a moral disparity between the accuser and the accused, the party imposing the sanctions and those whose speech is being sanctioned. It also suggests the existence of two well-defined groups: the righteous and the fallen. It is easy to see that antiracist proponents of the hate speech agenda set themselves up for counterattacks from alleged speakers of hate speech who, as we have seen, have four creative ways to undermine the morally superior position of antiracists. This discursive give-and-take reinforces the opposition between political factions and the impossibility of continued conversation about racism and hate speech.

Such opposition is maintained, in part, by competing speech codes and the code communities whose talk and identities they sustain. Social actors deeply invested in presenting oppositional identities thrive on competing cultural codes. It would be quite difficult to convince Hungarian antiracist advocates or their critics to opt out of the cultural codes they use to interpret the term "hate speech"—their public identities depend, to a large extent, on the consistent application of the rule. The danger of such opposition is that the original social issue of concern—namely, hate speech as a mode of public participation that further disadvantages already disadvantaged social groups—gets lost in the shuffle. And indeed, by 2006 the meaning of Hungarian "hate speech" had expanded to include any kind of derogatory public talk targeting any group.[26]

In *Steps to an Ecology of Mind*,[27] Gregory Bateson called the culturally based polarizing process I am describing here schismogenesis, the creation of division. Bateson is interested in how social division develops between a group defined by a shared set of cultural norms for conduct and another group defined by another set of norms.[28] Two cultural groups in conflict have three options: unity between the two groups, elimination of one or both groups, or dynamic equilibrium (peaceful coexistence) between the two groups. Schismogenesis between two groups takes place when in the course of interaction with each other the groups become locked in an interactional pattern that violates both groups' cultural norms. As a communicative pattern, schismogenesis can undermine equilibrium and propel groups toward symbolic or material destruction, and the cultural system they are parts of toward a breakdown. The tone versus content debate, the parliamentary debates about sanctions against hate speech, and resistance to the hate speech agenda are all examples and sites of schismogenesis. Debating and resisting *gyűlöletbeszéd* organizes Hungarian public speakers into groups that appear to be stuck in patterns of "we are right, you are wrong" or "we are righteous, you are evil," up to a point where there seems to be only limited, if any, consensus about, and interest in, the actual issue at hand. Hungarians are left with rampant verbal hygiene and no shared sense of verbal health.

Nonetheless, one can find examples of public expression on the Hungarian political scene that seem to acknowledge the destructive relationship between public talk surrounding hate speech and the resulting social divisions. Such public expression displays a commitment to eradicating derogatory public talk targeting historically disadvantaged minorities, and to move Hungarian public discourse from sustaining a state of schismogenesis to building a state of unity. I begin the next chapter with a cultural look at two possible courses of communicative action toward this end. As we venture from the domain of cultural knowledge into the realm of action, we also need to understand what happens when cultural thinking becomes politically committed and action-oriented.

6

FROM CULTURAL KNOWLEDGE TO POLITICAL ACTION

Having mapped the cultural terrain on which "hate speech" became such a hotly contested and debated issue in Hungary, it is time to ask: What can practitioners (politicians, policy analysts, activists, deliberation facilitators, concerned citizens, etc.) do with cultural knowledge? In what sense does cultural thinking lead to new forms of political action[1] in the form of public expression? Asking these questions reflects a commitment to an increasing number of communication scholars share, a commitment to the study of communication as a practical discipline with the capacity to address contemporary social problems.[2] I would like to end this book with reflections on three guises in which cultural knowledge is available to the political practitioner: as information, as counsel, and as a symbolic template for action.

Cultural Knowledge as Information

Let us imagine, for a moment, that a political practitioner with a particular interest in hate speech or a general interest in cultural thinking about political issues is leafing through this book. Chapters 1–5 present to him or her cultural knowledge as information. He or she is reading about the significance of tracing the history of a social issue's name, the diversity of meanings assigned to the issue, publicly enacted interpretations of that issue, and moralities (value systems founded on cultural beliefs) that render those interpretations sensible to the community of speakers. Or, we can imagine a political practitioner who has mastered and practiced the art of cultural thinking and cultural analysis and is now gazing at the cultural map of a social issue.

The cultural description and analysis of Hungarian *gyűlöletbeszéd* or any other social issue, as accurate as it may be, does not automatically translate into action. Knowing is not acting—having mapped a terrain does not mean having walked the terrain. It is true that cultural thinking and cultural analysis requires inter-action (interviews, casual conversations, etc.) with those who inhabit a cultural terrain. However, cultural thinking as understood in this book requires what Martín Carcasson calls passionate impartiality,[3] passion for the issue and politi-cal action, combined with an attitude of impartiality toward the political "sides" that take shape as the issue is publicly debated. Moments of cultural thinking require calming the desire to act, to take a stance, to contest, to judge. I chose the term "calming" instead of "extinguishing" for good reason: I doubt that the desire to act can be completely extinguished, especially when one is studying conten-tious social issues.

Contrary to contemporary critiques of adversary politics, the cultural thinker will quickly discover value in public utterances delivered in the heat of a polar-izing controversy. Heated debates that organize political actors into competing sides tell us about the genesis of social issues, and they can be a treasure trove of competing cultural histories, meanings, interpretations, and moralities. It would have been rather difficult to write this book if hate speech had not been such a divisive social issue in Hungary between 2000 and 2006. Adversary politics may not advance *solutions* to social issues, but it can certainly advance our under-standing of the cultural foundations of adversity and, ideally, offer clues about how political action can transcend adversity.

Cultural Knowledge as Counsel

Cultural thinking can help the practitioner achieve a nuanced understanding of a social issue's diverse meanings, the cultural foundations of those meanings, and insight into the local practices making use of that diversity and local moral systems informing political action. But we need not stop here. We can use cul-tural knowledge about a controversial, value-laden issue to chart novel, perhaps culturally unfamiliar courses of political action via public expression. This use of cultural knowledge is what I term "counsel," which can be generic and specific. Generic counsel is designed to inform particular genres of political action—in our case, public talk. Specific counsel is designed to inform politically motivated public expression with reference to a particular social issue, like hate speech in Hungary. Let us examine what forms generic and specific counsel can take in a case where adversary politics seems to have reached a stalemate and, as a conse-quence, the social distance between political actors appears to be widening and joint action targeting the issue seems less and less possible.

Generic Counsel

A basic premise of this book is that cultural thinking about a social issue, and the cultural analysis required by such thinking, can help us understand the complexity of histories, meanings, interpretations, and moralities brought into play in public talk about the issue. Combined with scholarship on rhetorical and deliberative practice, the cultural analysis presented in the preceding chapters yields generic counsel to practitioners of public expression with regard to participation in public debates. Such counsel, which affirms and expands the basic assumptions of cultural thinking discussed in the introduction to this book, can be summarized as the four C's: cultural claims, coherence of positions, contestation, and counterstrategy.

Cultural claims. In the process of adversarial debate, any claim about a focal issue (its history, meanings, interpretations, and its status as an actual social issue) is potentially grounded in a locally available moral system (a value or a set of values and underlying cultural premises) or a combination of locally available moral systems. To give an example from chapter 5, consider the claim that *gyűlöletbeszéd* is not an actual social issue, but rather that the term is an alien element of the Hungarian language, and that the political agenda built around it is an attempt to undermine Hungarian social order. This claim is partially grounded in the belief that a nation's language and social order exist in a mutually constitutive relationship, and therefore importing or coining "alien," "Orwellian" terms into political expression threatens "our" social order. Treating cultural claims as empirically testable statements of facts will not take the practitioner too far in understanding and speaking to the sociocultural logic informing those claims.

Coherence of positions. In chapter 5 we saw that even political views that may seem marginal or idiosyncratic at first can be supported by a widely shared, coherent set of values and beliefs. It is easy to dismiss the claim that hate speech is not an actual social issue in Hungary, as many conservatives and racists have done in the past. Much more patience is required to carefully reconstruct the cultural premises animating that claim. The effort, however, can pay off for the practitioner. Acknowledging and speaking to an audience's set of beliefs helps the speaker achieve partial identification and, through partial identification, persuasion. The speaker may adopt some opinions of the audience in order to alter others.[4]

Contestation. The meaning of social issues, especially of issues that come labeled with a single term (such as hate speech), can become the subject of essential contestation.[5] In this type of contest, participants vie for the control of an issue's meaning. Participants are motivated by competing values and social concerns, and they promote various interpretations of a given issue to position themselves on a plane of morality higher than that of their opponents. The debates discussed in chapters 3 and 4 illustrate this type of contestation (see tone vs. content, and human dignity vs. freedom of expression). Cultural thinking, when applied to cases of essential contestation, helps the practitioner temporarily establish a position of sense making from which no interpretation of a focal issue seems "right" or "wrong"; rather all interpretations are best seen as political moves to achieve control over the issue. Whether he or she desires to join or halt the contestation, understanding patterns of contestation may give the practitioner strategic advantage. Lakoff's analysis of political discourse in *Moral Politics*[6] or Goodall's *Counter-Narrative*,[7] for example, can be read as exercises in cultural thinking about the essential contestation of key social issues between the U.S. political left and right. Both authors are motivated by a desire to give strategic persuasive advantage to members of the political left.

Counterstrategy. Every argument implies a counterargument, and every rhetorical strategy bears within it the outlines of a counterstrategy.[8] There are two lessons to be drawn from the discussion of rhetorical strategy in chapter 5, a pessimistic one and an optimistic one. The pessimistic lesson is that, especially in rhetorical situations where the exigency is a pressing social issue, any rhetorical strategy can be met with a counterstrategy, and both of those strategies can be founded on equally coherent cultural logics. This is one of the main reasons why in public life representatives of opposing positions on social issues so often fall into "I'm right, you're wrong" or "I'm good, you're evil" patterns. The positive lesson is that the coexistence of strategies and counterstrategies does not preclude the possibility of a rhetorical escape from the interactional dynamic of "countering" and of advances toward joint action. It is not a necessity that the rhetorical strategies of two sides mirror each other (as in chapter 5). Again, a certain degree of identification with one's opponent as a rhetorical strategy can break the cycle created by both sides mirroring the other's strategy of creating interpretive and moral contrast and social division. Note that I am not suggesting that a public speaker should learn to rhetorically trick their opponents into believing they agree. Nor am I suggesting that identification with the other's views should be complete, or that one's beliefs and moral convictions should be thrown to the four winds. What I am suggesting is that the strategy of identification has the potential to disrupt deadlocked public conversations about pressing social issues.[9] New conversations taking shape in the wake of the disruption have the potential to disrupt deadlocked social divisions that came as a result of the strategy/counterstrategy pattern. New conversations can also create social situations in which participants do not necessarily agree or share cultural meanings, but rather see opportunities for advantageous joint action that does not violate their moral systems. Disruption does not guarantee unity—it cannot make lions lie with lambs—but disruption may bring to the surface concerns shared across cultural divides that serve as the basis for collaboration.

Specific Counsel

Generic counsel can be addressed to a community of speakers as a whole; specific counsel, on the other hand, is designed for a particular group of speakers or particular speakers within that community, and involves the evaluation of their actual speech performances. In order to make the move from the description and analysis of a particular issue to offering specific counsel, the cultural analyst must tread carefully. This move invites three types of consideration. First, evaluation sometimes implies critique.[10] It is helpful to distinguish two types of critique. Social actors setting out to alter habitual courses of action are generally motivated by dissatisfaction with the status quo. A cultural member's critique of communicative practices in his or her own community is what Donal Carbaugh calls natural criticism.[11] Cultural analysts often choose to simply report members' criticism of their community's practices. But it is possible, and sometimes advantageous, to go further: "Ethnographers have created a voice, a voice that assesses patterns within communities, patterns of contact with communities, patterns that ground communities. In each case, distance from the pattern is created in order to inspect it more reflectively, more closely, more critically. From such a stance, the practice and theory of communication can be enhanced. In creating these moments, the ethnographer adopts a voice of cultural criticism."[12]

In this section I combine the voices of cultural and natural criticism. The combination, however, requires the careful marking of the boundary between natural and cultural criticism. The dissolution of that boundary can easily lead to the misrepresentation of the ways of speaking and systems of meaning active in the way communal members conduct their daily lives. In order to attend to this boundary, I am compelled to clarify the ethical vantage point from which I formulate my cultural criticism. I believe that public talk has significant social consequences. Derogatory talk targeting historically disadvantaged (especially racial, ethnic, sexual, gender, and national) groups and their members has destructive power. (My reader will notice that here I am endorsing a content-oriented interpretation of hate speech.) In agreement with much contemporary political theory[13] and public deliberation scholarship,[14] I also believe in the generative and transformative power of public discourse. This set of beliefs informs some, but not all, Hungarian public talk about hate speech. I choose to offer specific counsel to those whose talk is informed by similar beliefs.

A second consideration is that cultural knowledge about communicative action does not automatically translate into expert, or even competent, social action in a given community of speakers. Individual communicative competence has two distinguishable components: knowledge of local communicative resources, and the ability to make use of those resources.[15] Those who study the possibility of using cultural knowledge to formulate and pursue social action argue that correctly understanding the meaning of conduct in a given cultural setting and engaging in locally meaningful conduct are two very different things.[16] Clifford Geertz reminds us that knowing how to wink is not winking, and knowing how to steal sheep is not sheep raiding.[17] In addition, cultural knowledge and the ability to act on such knowledge do not, by themselves, lead to expert conduct. The material of knowledge that cultural analysis can offer is words, and expert (effortless, intuitive, artful) conduct cannot be verbalized. The late Danish novelist Hans-Jørgen Nielsen writes with admiration about virtuoso soccer players (whom Danes refer to as *fodboldengel*, or "soccer angels"), whose art neither they nor anybody else can put into words, let alone teach.[18] The same applies to human interaction. The skills model of achieving competence in communication is a flawed representation of social reality because it underestimates the contingency and variability of interaction, a complexity that can be mastered only through careful cultivation in practice.[19]

Finally, and quite simply, the cultural analyst's suggestions for action should make sense to those members of the target community of speakers whom the analyst chooses to address. I do not mean that suggestions should be presented in the native language of the community, or that communal members can be expected to use them. Rather, suggestions should be heard as practicable responses to communal members' existing concerns. To this end I first identify existing Hungarian talk that authors social unity instead of social difference and division, and reflects a desire for forging a coalition of political actors against content-based hate speech. Next, I identify defining features of such talk. In the end, I suggest ways in which cultural knowledge as information and as generic advice can be used as resources to enhance the unifying potential of this type of talk.

The phrase "authoring unity" requires clarification. "Authoring unity" is a communicative practice that accomplishes the opposite of what Gerry Philipsen calls "authoring difference."[20] In an ethnographic case study, Philipsen discusses a casual, joking remark that the president of a university in the United States made at an awards banquet, in which he suggested that a Mexican-born student receiving an award at the event was an illegal immigrant. Philipsen argues that a cultural rule led the president to assume the liberty to place the student into an inferior social category, according to which "it is permissible to joke about the ethnicity or race of another person whom the speaker identifies as of a different race or ethnicity, when the occasion is defined as intimate."[21] Following this rule, the president appointed himself as an author of difference—a move that, unsurprisingly, many found objectionable.

Authors of unity do just the opposite: their talk suggests that they and other members of their social group share a social category with others who are commonly thought of as belonging to another category. Just as authoring difference does not create social difference in any observable, sociological sense, authoring unity does not create social unity. Nevertheless, these types of public talk are socially consequential because, through them, a speaker is able to express a position on how the social world works and how various categories of people relate to one another in it. The speaker's audience may find the expressed position natural, agreeable, or despicable, and they interpret the identity of the speaker and the legitimacy of their authorship accordingly. In addition, communication being "an unmatched resource for knowing one's world and acting within it,"[22] difference and unity authored by influential speakers can decisively shape the ways communal members relate to one another in their everyday lives.

In the Hungarian context, the term *gyűlöletbeszéd* and talk about *gyűlöletbeszéd* are typically used as resources for authoring moral and political difference. There are, however, notable exceptions. Some Hungarian public speech treats hate speech as a social issue and is designed for an audience that is likely to endorse or advocate interpretations of *gyűlöletbeszéd* different from the speaker's own. In what follows I examine and critique two instances of Hungarian talk where speakers seek to author unity in response to hate speech as a contentious social issue. The first type of talk expresses a desire to transcend endless political "debate"; the second proposes the creation of forums for a speech event marked by "dialogue."

If there is anything former prime minister Ferenc Gyurcsány will be remembered for in Hungary, it is his penchant for charismatic and risky rhetoric. In 2006, while still prime minister, he made international headlines by declaring to his fellow members of the Hungarian Socialist Party at a party retreat that his government "screwed things up" and that they had been "lying" to the citizens of Hungary for the past two years. After it was leaked, the speech sparked violent protests in cities around the country in the fall of 2006. The following year, on Holocaust Remembrance Day, Gyurcsány presented to the General Assembly of the Parliament his new "Zero Tolerance Proclamation" condemning racism and hate speech. In part of his twelve-minute speech he said the following:

Excerpt 6.1

Miniszterelnökként, politikusként megtanultam, hogy az ember követ el hibákat. Én is követtem el nem egyet politikusként és miniszterelnök-ként is. Van olyan, amelyet rosszallok, van olyan, amelyet szégyellek is. Van olyan, hogy az ember nem jól sáfárkodik mindazzal, amit rábíznak—megesik. Emberek vagyunk politikusként is. De mi van akkor, amikor átlépjük a végső határt, amikor már nem emberi hibákról, tévedésekről beszélünk, hanem a gonosszal való kokettálásról éppen saját magyarjaink ellenében? . . . Bár vitáink annyi van, mint a tenger, van egy pont, ahová ezt nem akarjuk elvinni. Abban közösek vagyunk, hogy nem kokettálunk rasszista, antiszemita, kirekesztő, intoleráns magatartással, nézetekkel, gondolatokkal, hogy annak még a látszatát is kerüljük, hogy mi ezt nem-csak hogy tűrjük, de talán még bátorítjuk is.

As prime minister and as a politician I learned that people make mis-takes. I made mistakes as a politician and as prime minister. Some of these mistakes I frown upon, others I am ashamed of. Sometimes one is not a good steward of what one had been entrusted with—such things happen. Politicians are human. But what happens when we cross the ultimate line between human mistakes and flirting with evil at the expense of our own Hungarians? . . . We [politicians] may have myriad differences of opinion but there should be a point beyond which our debates should not reach. What we all share is that we do not flirt with racist, anti-Semitic, discrimi-natory, intolerant behavior, views, and ideas, and we avoid even a sem-blance of tolerating or even encouraging these.[23]

Here the speaker attempts to author unity by envisioning a rhetorical situa-tion in which Hungarian politicians stand united against a commonly perceived rhetorical exigency, "racist, anti-Semitic, discriminatory, intolerant behavior, views, and ideas." A master rhetor, Gyurcsány makes use of five communicative resources to speak the language of unity. First, in this excerpt and throughout his speech he avoids using the term *gyűlöletbeszéd*, a term that, as we have seen in previous chapters, tends to be used to author moral and political difference in Hungarian public discourse. Second, he minimizes his moral authority as third-party judge of racism and hate speech by expounding on his own fallibility. Third, he places all members of his audience, politicians of all political stripes, into the basic social category of *ember* (translated here as "people" and "human"). Fourth, the phrase "our own Hungarians" (*saját magyarjaink*) evokes the sentiment of belonging to the nation of Hungary as a bounded social group, a sentiment we had seen articulated in the language of resistance against the hate speech agenda. Finally, he unites this group of humans against a common "evil," racism and hate speech.

Gyurcsány's speech is an excellent example of rhetorical identification with one's opponents, and of natural criticism targeting the politically and morally divided Hungarian political class. Despite this rhetorical tour de force, his speech, in the immediate context of the General Assembly meeting of April 16, 2007, seemed to fall flat. The publicly available video recording of the speech reveals that the response to the speech was applause among left-wing politicians—right-wing politicians appeared unmoved. Explaining this somewhat lukewarm response would require extensive analysis of the speech's social and political context. But two easily identifiable elements of that context provide clues as to why the speech did not prompt Hungarian politicians to close their ranks against hate speech. First, the speech was delivered only six months after the violent protests of 2006. By that time, Gyurcsány's political opponents had succeeded at undermining the prime minister's credibility and moral standing and branding him a compulsive liar.[24] Second, a mere ten minutes after the prime minister's speech ended a member of his party called on the General Assembly to not only sign the Zero Tolerance Proclamation but to support the bill criminalizing hate speech. The bill was a staple initiative of the Socialist Party. I surmise that one of the reasons the right-wing MPs, who were well aware that Gyurcsány's speech would be followed by such a bid,[25] did not respond more enthusiastically to the speech was that they concluded that the Socialists would use the universal values celebrated on Holocaust Remembrance Day to further their own political agenda.

This small episode from the life of the Hungarian Parliament brings into sharp relief the role of the third-party judge in public talk about hate speech, a topic I discussed in chapter 2. The third-party judge who assumes the "right" to identify and condemn hate speech inevitably places him- or herself under acute moral scrutiny. It is perhaps not an exaggeration to say that at the time of his speech Gyurcsány, with his tattered ethos, was probably the worst possible choice for third-party judge the left-wing government could produce. Thus Gyurcsány's speech is best described as "strategery," strategic communication based on a public influence model of communication according to which the key to persuasion is the well-designed message.[26] Such a view of communication fails to confront the radically context-bound nature of public interaction and rhetoric. For example, strategery assumes a neutral, passive audience. In Gyurcsány's case, this assumption could not be further from reality. Public speakers who wish to author unity must think carefully about the act of public expression as a social act, not as marketing. All relevant components of a speech event[27] in which the language of unity is to be spoken—such as the setting, the speaker and his or her audience, participants' communicative goals, the form and the content of what the speaker says, the sequence of public interaction, and the speech's tone and genre—must be given careful consideration.

I was able to observe a second way of authoring unity in the course of an ethnographic interview with the legal scholar Jenő Kaltenbach, who served as Parliamentary Commissioner for National and Ethnic Minority Rights from 1995 to 2007. Kaltenbach is a public figure who earned the respect of the Hungarian political class as a whole with his impeccable credentials and professionalism. I decided to interview him about Hungarian hate speech in part because of his reputation—to hold a political office for twelve consecutive years is a notable achievement in postcommunist Hungary!—and in part because of his professional interest in the issue.[28]

Prior to the part of the interview represented in excerpt 6.2, Kaltenbach was developing a natural critique of the Hungarian response to the issue of hate speech. He pointed out "a major deficiency of Hungarian public life," the lack of "expert dialogue" about constitutional legal issues, including hate speech. Such dialogue, he added, would require "some sort of a permanent forum" where "debate" could take place among representatives of relevant institutions.

Next, he turned to a related but different domain of political life that he thought could benefit from more dialogue: media representations of crimes committed by members of ethnic minorities. Toward the end of 2006, a gruesome murder took place in the village of Olaszliszka, news of which reverberated across the Hungarian media. A non-Romani man, Lajos Szögi, was driving through a Romani part of the village with his two daughters. Suddenly, a Romani girl ran across the street in front of his car and fell into the ditch on the opposite side of the road, startled but unscathed. Szögi stopped to check whether the girl was harmed but he had to retreat quickly into his car because the girl's relatives, who thought she was badly hurt or even dead, approached and threatened to kill him. Finally, Szögi was dragged from his car and beaten to death in front of his two daughters. The Romani perpetrators were given harsh sentences for manslaughter in May 2009. The case reignited the concern in the Hungarian press about both the social integration of Romanies and "Gypsy crime" (cigánybűnözés) as a subclass of criminal conduct committed by Romani people.

As Commissioner of National and Ethnic Minority Rights, the resurgence of this discussion alarmed Kaltenbach. The term "Gypsy crime" smacked of racism, he and his colleagues thought, because it identified ethnicity as the cause of criminal conduct. Kaltenbach took action: he contacted the National Association of Hungarian Journalists and called on them to officially condemn inciteful *cigányozás* (derogatory talk about Romani people) in the press, and the general tendency to discuss the Olaszliszka murder as an element of *cigányügy* (the Gypsy issue).[29] The association conducted an internal investigation and announced that they could not issue an official condemnation due to disagreement among their members and member organizations.[30] Kaltenbach also contacted the management of television channel TV2 and proposed a "televised expert dialogue." The dialogue, he suggested, could yield as its final product a set of shared, official ground rules for televised reporting on minorities.[31] Although TV2's management responded favorably, the televised dialogue did not take place.

The following excerpt is Kaltenbach's account of these events.

Excerpt 6.2

KALTENBACH: Ugye itt volt ez az olaszliszkai szörnyűség nem tudom . . .

AUTHOR: A gázolás?

KALTENBACH: Igen.

AUTHOR: És aztán a lincselés.

KALTENBACH: És az azt utána következő lincselés.

AUTHOR: Igen.

KALTENBACH: Na most ennek a sajtóvisszhangja rettenetes volt. Szóval legalábbis bizonyos sajtóorgánumok és bizonyos úgynevezett újságírók nem igazán nevezném őket ennek, vagy publicisták, szörnyű stílusban foglalkoztak a dologgal, mi ezt egyrészt szerepel az idei jelentésünkben elég terjedelmesen foglalkozunk ezzel, illetve ennek kapcsán a sajtó szerepével. Mert hiszen itt ugye a sajtónak a szerepe az óriási. És hát megpróbáltunk az üggyel úgy foglalkozni, nem mint igazából nem mint ombudsman hiszen konkrét hatáskörünk nem nagyon van ebben a dologban . . . de megpróbáltunk ezzel a dologgal hát nem ombudsman-szerűen foglalkozni éspedig úgy hogy párbeszédre hívtuk azokat a sajtóorgánumokat és általában az újságíró szakmát amelyik hát ezzel az üggyel foglalkozott és megítélésünk szerint nem úgy ahogy kellett volna. Hát volt egy-két levélváltás de ennél többre nem jutottunk. Tehát nem igazán sikerült, ma is nyitott ugye ez azóta jó pár hónap eltelt, ma is nyitott ma is nyitva van ez az ajtó, de a reakciók nagyon szerények. Tehát itt is megint a párbeszédre való készség hiánya figyelhető meg.

KALTENBACH: So there was that horror in Olaszliszka, I don't know [if you have heard about it] . . .
AUTHOR: The accident?
KALTENBACH: Yes.
AUTHOR: And then the lynching.
KALTENBACH: And the lynching after it.
AUTHOR: Yes.
KALTENBACH: Well, the press response to it was terrible. Some press organizations and some so-called journalists, I wouldn't necessarily call them that, let's call them columnists, wrote about this event using a horrible style of expression. We discussed this and the role of the press in a pretty detailed manner in our annual report from this year. Because of course the role of the press in this case is huge. And we tried to respond to this case not as parliamentary commissioner because the case falls beyond the boundaries of our jurisdiction . . . but we tried to respond to this case in a non-commissioner kind of capacity by initiating a dialogue with those press organizations and journalists in general who wrote about this case in a way that we thought was objectionable. Well, a couple of letters were exchanged but we hadn't gotten much further than that. We didn't succeed [at initiating a dialogue], many months have passed since, and this door remains open but the reactions [to our invitation] are minimal. This is yet another example of the total lack of willingness to engage in dialogue.[32]

Here "dialogue" is presented as an alternative to what a parliamentary commissioner normally does in cases that fall into his or her jurisdiction, namely, the formal investigation of human rights violations against particular individuals. The commissioner's office cannot investigate hate speech targeting an entire ethnic or racial minority.[33] The speaker here authors unity by suggesting (to the interviewer and to the Hungarian media) the possibility of a dialogue in response to hate speech. He describes dialogue as a type of speech situation that places those who hold potentially opposing views about hate speech into conversation with one another, a conversation that can lead to changed professional media practices. But a closer look at how the term "dialogue" is used here also reveals an ideal interactional sequence implied in the speaker's usage: (1) one party evaluates another party's professional conduct as morally objectionable; (2) the first party initiates a dialogue about the morally objectionable professional conduct with the second; (3) the two parties engage in a process of dialogue; (4) as a result of the dialogue, the second party alters its morally objectionable professional conduct in a way that is in agreement with the first party's moral system. One curious element of this formulation of the ideal of dialogue is that it presupposes a stark moral disparity between the two parties. The first party assumes the role of the third-party judge of hate speech and uses its moral authority to impose its interpretation on the second party. According to this model of dialogue, the second party has no choice but to acknowledge its own moral deficiency and to try its best to reconsider and reform its professional conduct following the first party's moral compass. The author of unity ends up authoring difference.

This notion of dialogue does not acknowledge that hate speech as a social issue is contested cultural terrain in contemporary Hungary. A speaker who wishes to author unity in response to hate speech must take into account that not only is there no agreement in Hungarian public discourse about why hate speech is a social issue, but some also question the status of hate speech as a social issue in the first place. Fixing the meaning of hate speech from the start means undermining the effort to author unity.

Another observation that should give us pause is the notable mismatch between the vision of dialogue presented in excerpt 6.2 and universally relevant features of dialogue. Craig identifies three domains of language use in which dialogue occurs: political/international dialogue, intergroup/societal dialogue, and individual dialogue.[34] All three domains share the normative requirements of mutual respect and openness to other views and change. A comparative study of the various meanings of dialogue and its equivalent terms in Blackfoot, Chinese, Hungarian, and Finnish indicates that two meanings of dialogue these languages share are an ethos of the mutuality of exchange and the potential for equality.[35] Dialogue, as used by Kaltenbach, assumes respect, openness, mutuality, and equality only in talk about the technical aspect of the proposed interaction (crafting the rules of professional conduct), but not about its moral aspect (the moral principles being translated into rules).

A final word of caution about Kaltenbach's vision of unity: Note that the range of participants Kaltenbach proposes to engage in dialogue includes only professionals and experts. Expert and professional public discourse about pressing issues tends to be technical and to not acknowledge competing values and meanings.[36] Hungarian hate speech as a social issue is saturated with competing moralities that deeply affect the nature of the issue itself. What the issue is, and whether the issue is an issue, are moral problems in the Hungarian context. I anticipate that expert discussions about hate speech are likely to run aground unless all experts around the table share an agreement about the meaning of hate speech. Even if they do agree on the issue, however, the decisions they make about the law or codes of professional conduct are not likely to be accepted by those who hold competing interpretations of the issue.

The deliberative democracy movement, which is currently gaining momentum in the United States,[37] may be able to provide an interesting communicative template for Hungarian authors of unity who wish to disrupt the polarizing public talk surrounding hate speech. Face-to-face deliberation had been defined as "(a) a process that involves the careful weighing of information and views, (b) an egalitarian process with adequate speaking opportunities and attentive listening by participants, and (c) dialogue that bridges differences among participants' diverse ways of speaking and knowing."[38] By expanding the range of participants to include not only experts and professionals but, for example, citizens who were affected by hate speech or had been cast as speakers of hate speech, Hungarians could explore new responses to public talk that places historically disadvantaged minorities into inferior social categories. Whether deliberation as a form of interaction could be sensibly and comfortably integrated into Hungarian ways of public speaking remains an empirical question. Deliberation is not democratic panacea, and its cultural fit is a critical question that ought not be sidestepped.[39]

Cultural Knowledge as Symbolic Template for Creative Action

In a 1975 poem titled "Some General Instructions," Kenneth Koch wrote:

> But *envy* is a good word
> To use, as *hate* is, and *lust*, because they make their point
> In the worst and most direct way, so that as a
> Result one is able to deal with them and go on one's way.[40]

What Koch says about hate applies to the Hungarian hate speech debate. "Hatred" and "hate speech" are good words for public speakers who want to deal with their opponents or adversaries quickly and go their own way. Allegations or competing interpretations of hatred and hate speech signal that the conversation between opponents is coming to an end and insurmountable difference shall reign. The danger inherent in this communicative pattern is that public debates concerned with the term "hate speech" can easily frustrate action designed to counter derogatory public expression targeting historically disadvantaged minorities. The social divisions that open up in the course of these debates undermine wide-scale joint

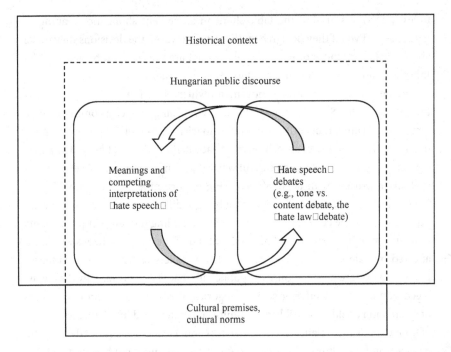

Figure 6.1   Categories of symbolic resources available to participants in the Hungarian "hate speech" debates

action. The divisions, I believe, can be closed or at least mitigated by speakers authoring unity—by means of culturally informed rhetoric, dialogue, or some other yet unrecognized form of public talk—in response to socially destructive public talk.

However, cultural analysis cannot tell the practitioner what to do. Cultural analysis is not speech writing, event planning, activism, policy analysis, blogging, or politicking. What cultural analysis *can* offer, however, are the ingredients of a symbolic template for creative communicative action. These ingredients are abstractions that "provide a template or blueprint for the organization of social and psychological processes, much as genetic systems provide such a template for the organization of organic processes."[41] Simply put, symbolic templates for communicative action ensure that such action remains meaningful from the perspective of one's cultural community.

The stuff of symbolic templates is symbolic resources. My primary goal in this book was to identify some of the most significant symbolic resources for participation in the Hungarian hate speech debates. Symbolic resources are best understood here as culturally sensible and appropriate ways of using the term "hate speech." In public expression, these ways of speaking function as communicative means to achieve desirable social, moral, and political ends. Symbolic resources identified in the book included meanings and competing interpretations of the term, various patterned, meaningful, public uses of the term, the cultural meanings that sustain such use, and the historical context of use. The relationships among these categories of symbolic resources are represented in figure 6.1. In the context of public discourse, public debates about hate speech mobilize meanings and competing interpretations of the term while these meanings and interpretations render competing positions sensible to participants. Cultural premises ground competing positions in widely shared cultural beliefs, and cultural norms stake out appropriate courses of action that follow from those premises. Finally, the historical context of the debates offers participants a range of historical facts they can draw on to build rhetorical strategies and arguments. The permeable borderline between historical context and public discourse represents the observation that some historical facts, or their meaning and significance with relation to other historical facts, are the outcome of public conversations or debates about them. The two competing histories of the meaning of hate speech in the tone versus content debate (chapter 3) are examples of how public expression strategically shapes the relevant historical context.

Any social issue, anywhere in the world, at any historical moment, can be made the object of cultural thinking. It is up to the practitioner to use cultural resources to craft unfamiliar, yet sensible and efficacious, courses of action based on new combinations of existing symbolic templates. I should note that the practitioner is not alone in the quest for creative and competent action. A group of professionals standing by and waiting for practitioners' calls for help are design specialists trained to both recognize the difference between culturally competent and incompetent social action and recommend novel modes of engagement.[42]

Social issues have names, they are talked about in a variety of ways, and the form and meaning of those names and that talk vary across cultural groups. Overlooking the communicative and cultural aspects of social issues means blinding ourselves to the complex and interesting lives these issues live among us. Inevitably, tackling social issues requires careful attention to how those issues are talked into, and out of, being.

APPENDIX: THEORY AND METHODS

According to a traditional, received vision of ethnography, the ethnographic process looks something like this: an ethnographer arrives in an alien cultural community living in an easily identifiable geographic locale or site, spends at least a year in that community interacting with the "natives" and typing up reams of field notes, and then returns to where he or she came from to write scholarly articles or monographs about the natives' ways. The ethnographic project that this book is founded on differed from this vision in significant ways. First, the cultural community I studied was my own. Second, my interest centered on publicly spoken words, and not on the speakers. The present book is primarily an ethnography of the use of a Hungarian term, not of Hungarians. To borrow an idea from George Marcus,[1] I did not follow people, I followed a term. Inevitably, I did end up learning quite a bit about Hungarians from the ways they used language in public settings. Third, as a result of the choice to follow *gyűlöletbeszéd*, I did not need a particular research site, nor did I need to be physically present in Hungary for a full year. My field site was the Hungarian public sphere between 2000 and 2006, a site with no geographic boundaries. I chose to conduct participant observation and interviews in Budapest for the sake of convenience. As a Budapest native I was familiar with the city, and, Budapest being the capital, I had easy access to Hungary's political elite and the country's equivalent of the Library of Congress, the National Széchenyi Library. In addition, the Internet allows the ethnographer to track the travels of a political term on a cultural terrain from a distance—in my case, the United States.

The Ethnography of Communication

The ethnography of communication (EC),[2] the research tradition that inspired this book, is primarily interested in investigating the relationship between communication and culture. More particularly, ethnographers working in this tradition are interested in how and for what purposes language is used in particular communities of speakers,[3] in particular types of social situations, in a way that

seems sensible and appropriate to communal members. EC scholars see communication as patterned, context-bound language use, and culture as local systems
of meanings (the symbolic properties of various units of language use, and the
norms guiding and the premises informing that use). Patterned, observable acts
of communication are seen both as shaped by culture and as the "location" of
culture's existence.

EC developed its own methods of qualitative inquiry. The analytic framework
I make use of in this book is cultural discourse analysis (CuDA).[4] The following
assumptions outline a general approach to language and culture in the context of
the cultural discourse analysis of Hungarian *gyűlöletbeszéd*.

*The various meanings of the use of the term are recoverable from actual written,
spoken, or drawn discourse.* Ethnographers of communication maintain that an
empirical argument always takes precedence over an ideological one.[5] Like other
research traditions interested in explaining the foundations of social interaction,
ethnographers of communication puzzle over "the commonplace and seemingly
unremarkable fact that people mean something by what they say and that their
meaning is recoverable from what they say by the people they address."[6] The
Hungarian cultural logic of using the term "hate speech" is best derived from
the analysis of actual Hungarian utterances, texts, or graphic representations.
An analytic assumption at work here is that utterances, texts, and graphic representations gathered from other cultural communities that make use of the term
"hate speech" would yield cultural logics that do not necessarily resemble the
Hungarian one.[7]

*Any written or spoken use of the term can be regarded as communicative action
in which the term functions as a communicative resource.* In the tradition of EC,
all types of language use count as the use of locally available resources for communication. Any example of language use can be regarded evidence of the speaker's "access to and command of resources for speaking,"[8] unless the speaker's
audience refuses to recognize it as intelligible. It follows that hate speech in the
Hungarian context can be viewed not only as a term but also as a term-for-talk,
a resource particular speakers use for the purpose of accomplishing a range of
communicative goals.

*Any use of the term is a goal-oriented mobilization of a communicative resource
in a particular community of speakers.* The analyses presented in this book are
partly based on the assumption that *gyűlöletbeszéd* is a term used in ways that
appear intelligible and motivated to a community of speakers. As a result, a single
mention of *gyűlöletbeszéd* can be analyzed as meaningful in that moment and
across communicative moments. In the moment, the use of the term is an act
designed for a particular recipient or group of recipients. Across moments, the

use of the term offers clues to the ethnographer about how a communally recognized resource is being utilized.

As a communicative resource, the recurrent use of the term constitutes a patterned communicative practice across multiple contexts within the community. EC assumes that any recurring utterance is potentially a social practice. The concept of practice implies repeated, conventionalized action. Action, as Sanders puts it, is "behavior that is interpreted as being produced for the sake of its functionality."[9] "A behavior," he adds, "counts as an action if it produces a change in or contributes to a material or social state or conditions (e.g., by means of the behavior, a computer is switched on; by means of the behavior, an invitation is issued or accepted), and if the behavior is interpreted as having been produced with the intention of having that effect on a current state or condition."[10] Hate speech in Hungarian public discourse can be shown to operate in such a way: its use is designed to promote moral or political agendas, and its use is understood as morally or politically motivated.

As patterned practice, the use of the term carries a variety of context-dependent meanings. The approach to communication outlined here joins other approaches to language use that view meaning as radically shaped by a variety of contexts and contextual features.[11] Ethnography of communication views and interprets communication practices with relation to any and all elements of any and all contexts that appear relevant to the participants of a given communicative situation. This range of contextual features includes the physical setting; speakers' and audience members' social roles and identities; the communicative ends of present or non-present speakers and audiences; the sequence of communicative acts into which an utterance is inserted; the tone or emotional pitch of the practice; the channel or channels of communication used; relevant norms for the production and interpretation of the practice; locally recognized communicative genres, texts, prior or anticipated utterances, small or large-scale social dramas, and so on. What further complicates the ethnographer's project is that the commitment to understand meaning-in-context means that the analytic line separating a meaningful utterance from its relevant contexts becomes blurry. Such blurring, however, and the attention to a broad range of contexts are often necessary to achieve subtlety and richness of cultural description.[12]

As meaningful practice, the use of the term implies cultural discourses. The cultural discourse concept captures the coherent and ordered character of culturally variable expressive systems. Ethnographic interest in cultural discourse originated from a theoretical concern with the language–culture relationship. Ethnographers of communication challenge theories of this relationship according to which language reflects culture, culture determines language, or that language, in some sense, *is* culture. Sherzer discussed discourse as "the nexus, the actual and concrete expression of the language–culture–society relationship," which "includes and relates both textual patterning (including such properties as coherence and disjunction) and a situating of language in natural contexts of use."[13] Cultural discourses are *cultural* because they are specific to certain speech communities, *social* because they shape local enactments of social order, and *linguistic* because they exist in and inform patterned, context-bound, rule-governed uses of language. Carbaugh and his associates argued that CuDA's attention to the relationship between social interaction and culture brings into view participants' conditions for meaningful social activity. These conditions can be formulated as cultural premises, which in turn help the researcher understand "the meaningfulness of communication to participants, and the ways these meanings are socially negotiated through the symbolic practices of particular social scenes." Cultural premises are formulations of what participants need to know and believe to make sense of and utilize cultural discourses. The meanings of these discourses encompass basic premises about identity, communicative action, social relations, feeling, and the environment in which speakers conduct their daily lives.[14] The cultural discourse concept posits a strong, mutually constitutive relationship between language and culture, but it does not suggest that the two are the same.

More than one cultural discourse can inform the use of the term. It is a fallacy to assume that a practice (e.g., the use of *gyűlöletbeszéd* in Hungary) cannot be informed by multiple cultural discourses within the same community of speakers. EC recognizes the possibility of competing meanings within the same community of speakers but also calls attention to the fact that competing meanings are often shared—that is, understood as competing meanings—by members of the community.[15]

Within CuDA, the analytic framework I used to structure my ethnographic research project was terms-for-talk analysis,[16] which is explained and demonstrated in chapter 2. Other analytic strategies used to make sense of the ways Hungarians make sense of hate speech are discussed in the analytic chapters (chapters 2–5). Next, I review the types of primary and supplementary materials I collected for analysis between January 2004 and May 2007.

Broadcast Talk About "Hate Speech"

Using Internet searches for the term *gyűlöletbeszéd* I was able to identify seventeen broadcast episodes featuring such talk. The sources of broadcast talk are listed in tables A.1, A.2, and A.3. I collected these broadcasts from three types of sources: television (twelve episodes) and radio (three episodes) broadcasts and webcasts (two episodes). Episodes were either legally downloaded from the Internet or purchased from broadcasting companies.[17]

In the course of my fieldwork I had to acknowledge that hate speech as a social issue was supercharged with politics. In order to avoid the accusation of political bias in the selection of broadcast episodes, I sampled episodes from programs associated with the political left (e.g., the political talk shows *A szólás szabadsága* and *Nap-Kelte*) and the political right (e.g., the political talk shows *Kérdések órája* and *Sajtóklub*), and from programs considered politically neutral (e.g., the satirical news analysis outlet *Pilóta Rádió*). My analysis is based on all these episodes, but only a handful of turns at talk made it into my representation of Hungarian hate speech debates in this book. Such is the nature of ethnographic representation: the lion's share of analysis is carried out behind the scenes.

I found it necessary to establish a set of criteria for identifying broadcast episodes where discussions about hate speech took place. In the case of most episodes, broadcasters clearly marked the episodes' beginning and end. The most frequently used means of such marking were the explicit framing of hate speech

Table A.1   Television data inventory

Title	Channel	Date	Abbreviation
A szólás szabadsága (The freedom of expression)	M1	April 22, 2007	ASZSZ1
A szólás szabadsága (The freedom of expression)	M1	November 16, 2003	ASZSZ2
Az este (The evening)	M1	May 24, 2004	AE
Kérdések órája Csintalan Sándorral (An hour of questions with Sándor Csintalan)	HírTV	July 26, 2005	KÓ
Nap-Kelte (Sunrise)	M1	July 19, 2005	NK1
Nap-Kelte (Sunrise)	M1	August 9, 2005	NK2
Nap-Kelte (Sunrise)	M1	April 18, 2007	NK3
Sajtóklub (Press club)	Budapest TV	June 25, 2003	S1
Sajtóklub (Press club)	Budapest TV	July 2, 2003	S2
Sajtóklub (Press club)	Budapest TV	September 3, 2003	S3
Sajtóklub (Press club)	Budapest TV	May 21, 2004	S4
Sajtóklub (Press club)	Budapest TV	May 28, 2004	S5

Table A.2   Radio data inventory

Title	Station	Date	Abbreviation
Aréna (Arena)	InfoRádió	July 18, 2005	A
Szóljon hozzá! (Have your say!)	Kossuth Rádió–MR1	September 24, 2003	SZH
Tizenhat óra (4 p.m.)	Kossuth Rádió–MR1	May 27, 2006	TÓ

Table A.3   Webcast data inventory

Title	URL	Date	Abbreviation
Pilóta rádió (Radio pilot)	http://worluk.index.hu/pilota/pilot2.mp3	January 13, 2004	PR1
Pilóta rádió (Radio pilot)	http://worluk.index.hu/pilota/pilot3.mp3	December 29, 2003	PR2

as the focus of discussion, displaying the term "hate speech" on the bottom of the screen in televised episodes, or the use of "hate speech" in the headings of transcripts released by broadcasting companies. In the case of less clearly bounded episodes, I looked for discursive cues speakers used to introduce hate speech as the focal topic of the discussion and to later shift to a different topic.

The length of episodes constituting the primary data varied from three to fifty-three minutes. I was able to legally download transcripts of some broadcasts, and I fully transcribed the remaining episodes myself. Downloaded transcripts were often inaccurate representations of actual broadcast speech, and I took special care to correct them. As I was interested in the use of words, phrases, and concepts, I transcribed broadcasts at the word level, noting repetition but not *uhs*, *ums*, pauses, overlaps, and so on. My broadcast materials listed in tables A.1, A.2, and A.3 yielded ninety-three pages of transcripts.

Field Notes

I spent nine months[18] in Budapest conducting participant observation and interviews. I observed public events where I expected to hear discussions or at least mentions of hate speech, and events where the organizers were commonly seen as speakers of hate speech. I jotted down observations during these events and

Table A.4 Observed public events

Date and location of event	Type of event	Purpose of event	Organizers/sponsors
February 13, 2004; Budapest, Dísz Square	Demonstration	Commemoration of the fifty-ninth anniversary of the liberation of Budapest; to protest recent events associated with racism and discrimination	Magyar Ellenállók és Antifasiszták Szövetsége (Alliance of Hungarian Partisans and Anti-Fascists), Párbeszéd Budapestért Alapítvány (Dialogue for Budapest Foundation), Civil Fórum (Civic Forum), Nagy Imre Társaság (Imre Nagy Society), Otthont Magyarországból Összefogás (Let's Make Hungary Our Home! Coalition)
February 14, 2004; Budapest, Heroes' Square	Demonstration	Commemoration of the death of Hungarian and German soldiers on February 14, 1945, during the Siege of Budapest	Vér és Becsület Kulturális Egyesület (Blood and Honor Cultural Association), Lelkiismeret '88 Csoport (Conscience '88 Group), regional skinhead groups
March 14, 2004; Budapest, Petőfi Square	Demonstration	Commemoration of the Hungarian Revolution of 1848	Vér és Becsület Kulturális Egyesület (Blood and Honor Cultural Association)
March 21, 2004; Budapest, Millenáris	Public debate and reading	Discussion of antiracism charters and of racism in Hungary and beyond (title: "Eszközök a rasszizmus ellen" [Tools against racism])	Friedrich Naumann Alapítvány (Friedrich Naumann Foundation), Magyar Rádió (Hungarian Radio)
April 4, 2004; Budapest, Szabadság Square	Demonstration	Protest against the Soviet memorial statue located in the square	Lelkiismeret '88 Csoport (Conscience '88 Group), Hatvannégy Vármegye Ifjúsági Mozgalom (Sixty-Four Counties Youth Movement), Magyar Nemzeti Front (Hungarian National Front), Jobbik Magyarországért Mozgalom (Movement for a Better Hungary)
April 16, 2004; Budapest, Ráday Street	Public lecture	On far-right activism in Hungary	Szabad Demokraták Szövetsége, IX. kerületi szervezet (Alliance of Free Democrats, 9th district chapter)

April 17, 2004; Budapest, Hungarian Academy of Sciences	Conference	International Holocaust studies conference (title: "The Holocaust in Hungary: Sixty Years Later")	Holokauszt Dokumentációs Központ és Emlékgyűjtemény Közalapítvány (Holocaust Documentation Center and Memorial Collection Public Foundation)
February 28, 2007; Budapest, Szent János military hospital, Buda Castle	Play	Performance of the play *Hagen, avagy a gyűlöletbeszéd* (Hagen, or hate speech) by the Hungarian playwright János Térey	Krétakör Színház (Chalk Circle Theater)
March 12, 2007; Budapest, Stefánia mansion	Public meeting	Meeting of the National Committee of the Alliance of Hungarian Partisans and Anti-Fascists	Magyar Ellenállók és Antifasiszták Szövetsége (Alliance of Hungarian Partisans and Anti-Fascists)
March 12, 2007; Budapest, Hegyvidéki Liberal Club	Public meeting	Conversation with former president of the Alliance of Free Democrats Gábor Kuncze	Hegyvidéki Liberális Klub (Liberal Club of Hegyvidék)
March 15, 2007; Vörösmarty Square	Demonstration	Commemoration of the Hungarian Revolution of 1848	Jobbik Magyarországért Mozgalom (Movement for a Better Hungary)
March 20, 2007; Berzsenyi Dániel secondary school	Public debate	Public debate between János Kóka and Gábor Fodor, candidates for party leader of the Alliance of Free Democrats	Szabad Demokraták Szövetsége (Alliance of Free Democrats)
May 10, 2007; Danube Wharf below the Parliament building	Demonstration	Commemoration of the end of World War II; protest against racism and discrimination	Magyar Szocialista Párt (Hungarian Socialist Party)

Table A.5   Visits to public lectures sponsored by the Vér és Becsület Kulturális
Egyesület (Blood and Honor Cultural Association)

Year	Locations	Dates
2004	Kis Olimpia, 11th district, 63 Tétényi Avenue	March 28, April 25, May 20
2007	Pannon GMK, 7th district, 42 Péterfy Sándor Street	February 25, March 11, March 25, April 22, May 6

wrote up detailed field notes later. Tables A.4 and A.5 list all the public events I
attended.

My choice to observe the public meetings of the Blood and Honor Cultural
Association (BHCA), a pro-Nazi group, is a methodological response to the
dominant view of hate speech in Hungary. In Hungarian public discourse and
social science scholarship, hate speech is most often associated with far-right
ideologies such as nationalism and various forms of discrimination, particularly
xenophobia and racism.[19] The National Security Office, which regularly tracked
the activities of BHCA, listed the organization as a bona fide far-right group.[20]
BHCA struck me as a collective that fit the dominant description of a racist group
whose members routinely speak hate speech. The public lecture series they organized was advertised on the Internet and was easily accessible for nonmembers.[21]
Between fifteen and thirty-five skinheads and political sympathizers attended
each lecture, which lasted sixty to seventy-five minutes. At the end of the fieldwork period, the combined length of my field notes was 124 single-spaced pages.

Ethnographic Interviews

During my stay in Budapest I conducted ten semi-structured, face-to-face interviews. I identified interviewees using two criteria: my interviewees were either
widely recognized public figures who had expressed robust views about hate
speech or had been accused of hate speech, or they were politically active and
thus had firsthand insight into the interactional dynamics of public talk about
the issue. Six interviewees fell into the first category, four into the second. All
interviews were conducted in Hungarian. Contrary to my expectations, interviewees readily made themselves available despite the politically sensitive nature
of the topic. The interview guide I used to partially structure the conversation
included the following questions:

- Can you recall an example of hate speech you have encountered in Hungary? Please recall this instance in as much detail as possible.
- Who else do you think would characterize this utterance as an example of hate speech? Who would resist such a characterization? Why?
- Why would you characterize this utterance as hate speech? What is hateful about it? What other events would you characterize as such, and on what basis?
- If you were to publicly characterize this utterance as hate speech, what would be the consequences? What would your colleagues/subordinates/superiors/party members/constituents/political opponents say?
- How would you describe the social significance of calling certain utterances or types of talk hate speech? Who is it important for, and why? Who do you think believes this is unimportant, and why?
- Do you think there is anything that needs to be done about hate speech? If you think so, and if you had a chance to do something about hate speech, what would you do? Why? If you don't think so, why?
- Do you think that the practice of characterizing certain acts of speaking as hate speech in Hungary is unique, or is it pretty much done like in other countries where hate speech is a topic of concern?
- Do you think people will still talk about hate speech in Hungary in ten/twenty/fifty years? Who will talk about it, and why?

I did not follow this guide in a linear fashion during interviews. Rather, I used the guide as a mnemonic device to make sure that interviewees addressed all aspects of the use of hate speech in which I was interested.

Newspaper Articles

I collected 487 articles from the Hungarian press using Internet searches of the term *gyűlöletbeszéd*. I had online access to almost all these articles, with the exception of seventeen articles in the daily newspaper *Népszabadság* from 1996, which I obtained from the archives of the National Széchenyi Library in Budapest. I pulled articles from sources associated with the political left (e.g., *Népszabadság, Népszava*), the political right (e.g., *Magyar Nemzet*), and sources widely considered politically neutral (e.g., *Index*). The full collection of articles consisted of approximately five hundred single-spaced pages.

Meeting Transcripts

I also collected transcripts of eight parliamentary committee meetings where hate speech was discussed. At the end of 2003, three standing committees of the Hungarian Parliament (the Constitutional, Judicial, and Standing Orders Committee, the Committee on Human Rights, Minorities, Civil, and Religious Affairs, and the Committee on Culture and the Media) were given the task to deliberate about a bill (No. T/5179) designed to render hate speech a criminal offense. I identified twenty-two pages of the official transcripts where the bill was the focus of deliberation among the MPs present.

Political Cartoons

Finally, I collected twenty-eight political cartoons depicting hate speech. The cartoons I identified used either the term *gyűlöletbeszéd* or a related native term for communicative action in their captions, or were published alongside a newspaper or magazine article discussing hate speech or a related term. In order to identify relevant cartoons, I surveyed my collection of newspaper articles on hate speech and collected ten cartoons. I also conducted a focused search of the daily newspaper *Népszabadság*, which publishes an above-average number of political cartoons. I concentrated on those issues of the paper that featured coverage of the Hegedűs affair (see chapter 1) between August 2001 and December 2003. The National Széchenyi Library gave me permission to digitally photograph eighteen cartoons from the print edition of he paper.

NOTES

INTRODUCTION

1. This is not to say that these ideals and evils are not in any way anchored in the material world. They are.
2. Allport 1954.
3. Butler 1997.
4. Lakoff 2000.
5. Matsuda, Lawrence, Delgado, and Crenshaw 1993.
6. Smitherman-Donaldson and van Dijk 1988.
7. Walker 1994.
8. Ibid., 14.
9. See, for example, Béres and Horányi 1999.
10. Fodor 2004.
11. Szabó 2006b.
12. Szabó 2006a.
13. Agar 1980.
14. Hymes 1974.
15. Hymes 1972.
16. See Downs 2006.
17. Geertz 1983, 16.
18. Agar 1994.

CHAPTER 1

1. See Craig and Tracy 2005; Goodwin 2002.
2. See https://orszaginfo.magyarorszag.hu/informaciok/kultura/sajto.html for data from 2010.
3. See Gal 1991, 1994, 1995; Harper 2006, 2007.
4. For key studies of anti-Semitism and anti-Semitic public discourse in Hungary, see Bibó 1948/1986, chap. 19; Braham 1981; Dési, Gerő, Szeszlér, and Varga 2004; Gerő, Varga, and Vince 2001, 2002; Gyurgyák 2001; Karsai 1992; Králl 1994; Kubinszky 1976; Pelle 2001; and Vértes 1997.
5. For key studies of anti-Romani sentiment, see, for example, Babusik 2005; Barany 2002; Bernáth 2000, 2002, 2005; Daróczi and Bársony 2004; Kállai and Törzsök 2000, 2002, 2003, 2004, 2006; Katz 2005; Kemény 1999; Neményi and Szalai 2005; Törzsök, Paskó, and Zolnay 2007, 2008.
6. Hankiss 2007.
7. Turner 1969.
8. Hankiss 2007, 8.

9. Tellér 1996, 52.

10. See Gombár and Volosin 2005.

11. Láng 2011.

12. "Der Brokerskandal" 2004.

13. Tellér 1996.

14. Tamás 2007.

15. Pogonyi 1996.

16. In the course of an e-mail exchange, Csepeli explained to me that during his years of research work in the United States he was influenced by Austin's (1962) speech act theory, Allport's (1954) notion of antilocution, or prejudiced talk, as the first step toward racially motivated violence, and the campus speech codes debate of the 1990s.

17. The "violation of human dignity," as we will see in chapter 4, is a cornerstone of Hungarian constitutional scholarship on human rights.

18. Pál 2006, 2011.

19. Halmai 1994, chap. 4.

20. Györgyi 2003.

21. Tellér 1996.

22. See chapter 4 for additional discussion of the Constitutional Court's decisions pertaining to hate speech.

23. *Schenck v. United States*, 249 U.S. 47 (1919).

24. Turner 1980.

25. Philipsen 1987, 252.

26. Reference to the Compromise of 1867 that created the Austro-Hungarian Empire.

27. "Galician vagrants": Jews.

28. "People of yore": *óemberek*, people of the Old Testament, of the pre–New Testament moral order.

29. "Culmination": *magaslat*, literally "height" or "highland."

30. Endre Ady (1877–1919): Hungarian poet.

31. Hegedűs 2001. The linguistic style of the text feels somewhat archaic and pompous to the Hungarian native speaker. Also, note that Hegedűs used capitalized print in the original Hungarian text.

32. The prosecution of public figures because of hate speech is not a uniquely Hungarian practice. Recent widely publicized examples from other countries include the prosecution of the South African politician Julius Malema, the British fashion designer John Galliano, and the Dutch politician Geert Wilders.

33. Turner 1980.

34. Philipsen 1987.

35. Turner 1980, 167.

36. Hankiss 2007. .

37. Numbered excerpts contain communication data I analyze. Unnumbered excerpts provide the sociocultural context for, or illustration of, arguments throughout the book. The original Hungarian language has been included in the text to increase the transparency of my analysis, and to remind the reader that the object of my analysis is the original Hungarian language use, and not its English translation. All uncredited translations from Hungarian into English are mine.

38. Dzindzisz 2001.

39. The caller was implying that the socialists had lied to the Hungarian public, and equated politicians' misleading statements with hate speech.

40. Újhelyi 2003.

41. Megyeri 2003.

42. Krajczár 2002.

CHAPTER 2

1. Philipsen 1992; Carbaugh 1989; Carbaugh, Berry, and Nurmikari-Berry 2006.
2. Carbaugh, Gibson, and Milburn 1997; Carbaugh 2007.
3. Sherzer 1987.
4. *SZH*, September 24, 2003, P2, 11:17. Data sources are identified in the appendix. See tables A1–A3.
5. *TÓ*, May 27, 2006, P2, 27:49.
6. *SZH*, September 24, 2003, P2, 19:33.
7. Ibid., 8:29.
8. The transcript of the conversation was published in Kovács 2004.
9. Jobbik's message was that people should reject the commercialism of the Christmas holiday and remind themselves of its religious origin and meaning.
10. "Huszonöt napra" 2005.
11. "Harminc napra" 2004.
12. "Kizárják" 2004.
13. "Tilos-ügy" 2004; "Az ügyészség szerint" 2004.
14. "Harminc napra" 2004.
15. Spirk 2004.
16. This particular slogan is an ironic appropriation of the name of a leftist social movement initiated by Hungarian sociologist Zsuzsa Hegedűs in 1992. The movement organized rallies to alert the public to the growing political influence of the Hungarian extreme right in the wake of the 1989 regime change (Bálint 2000). In 2005, Hegedűs criticized conservatives for "abusing" the name of the movement ("Visszaélnek" 2005).
17. "Atrocitásokba torkollott" 2004.
18. The video recording of the speech was retrieved from http://www.hirtv.hu/.
19. "Bűnös" 2004.
20. See, for example, Németh 1939/1992, 895–96.
21. Gerő 2007.
22. The choice of the term "third-party judge" reflects the observation that in the overwhelming majority of Hungarian cases reviewed for this research, judges did not self-identify as a member of the group targeted by *gyűlöletbeszéd* in the communicative situation in which the judgment was made.
23. One exception to this rule is parody. In some rare cases, I have seen a speaker take the role of a third-party judge and evaluate one of their own utterances as hate speech. This kind of role play tended to serve the purpose of parodying a real or hypothetical third-party judge's moral status or use of the term "hate speech." The infamous Hungarian political blogger Tomcat performed such parody by titling one of his blog entries "Gyűlöletbeszélek" (I am hate-speaking) (Tomcat 2004).
24. *SZH*, September 24, 2003, P2, 3:20.
25. The caller's use of the form *két gyűlöletbeszéd* (two hate speeches) is unusual.
26. Traditional Hungarian kindergartens organize children into three age groups: small, middle, and big.
27. *NK1*, July 19, 2005, 07:31.
28. Hymes 1962, 19.

CHAPTER 3

1. Tannen 1999.
2. Hutchby 1996, 2005.

3. Scannell 2000 12.

4. Sometimes "tone" was discussed as "style" (*stílus*), but the two terms were used interchangeably. I prefer "tone" to "style" because the former was used more often.

5. Philipsen 1997, 2002.

6. Carbaugh 1988/1989.

7. Carbaugh 1988, 1996.

8. Carbaugh 1996.

9. Ibid., 124.

10. Philipsen 1992.

11. Coutu 2000, 2008.

12. Boromisza-Habashi 2010.

13. "Megbeszéljük" 2004.

14. The Arrow Cross Party was a Hungarian national socialist political movement built around the so-called Hungarist ideology. The party's leader, Ferenc Szálasi, served as "Leader of the Nation" from 1944 to 1945 with Hitler's support.

15. "Megbeszéljük" 2004.

16. This adversarial mirroring move can be glossed like this: "That you charge someone with hate speech is itself a form of hate speech because you obviously hate/discriminate against those whom you are charging with hate speech."

17. The cultural analysis of the tone side of the debate builds exclusively on words spoken or written by András Gerő. This reflects an analytic choice. Although Gerő was not the only participant of the debate who used a tone-oriented interpretive strategy, his use of this resource was the most articulate and, therefore, ripest for analysis.

18. The year 1989 was when democratic change occurred in Hungary.

19. My translation here mirrors the original Hungarian sentence construction to preserve an act of political correctness by the author. The word *diák* (student) in Hungarian usage has a recognized, if slightly archaic, connotation of "male student." To point out that not only the *diákok* (students/male students) but also the *diáklányok* (female students) are protected by self-regulation indicates the recognition of the traditional gender-biased use of the term *diák*.

20. Tamás 2004.

21. Gerő 2004.

22. "Hate narrative" is not a widely recognized term for talk in the Hungarian context.

23. "Megbeszéljük" 2004.

24. Eörsi 2004.

25. See Pál (2011) for a more general discussion of identity work done in the context of Hungarian hate speech debates.

26. Baxter 1993.

27. Ibid., 324.

28. Zelki 2004.

29. György 2004.

30. Varga 2004.

31. "Megbeszéljük" 2004. The term *háziszerző* implies that (1) the intellectuals labeled with the term are too closely, even exclusively, associated with *Élet és Irodalom* and form a sort of loyal clique; and (2) as members of that clique, they do not entertain the possibility of expressing ideas that are not in perfect alignment with the radical liberal ideology of the magazine.

32. Cameron 1995.

33. Ibid., 17.

34. Kulick and Schieffelin 2004.

CHAPTER 4

1. Geertz 1983, chap. 8.
2. Downs 1985.
3. Downs 2006.
4. Geertz 1983, 222.
5. Nielsen 2004.
6. Smith and Loudiy 2005.
7. Carbaugh 1990.
8. Yankah 1998.

9. EMB/35/2003, Committee on Human Rights, Minorities, Civil, and Religious Affairs proceedings, October 28, 2003. All committee meeting transcripts are available from the Library of the General Assembly. See http://www.ogyk.hu/.

10. AIB/38/2003, Constitutional, Judicial, and Standing Orders Committee proceedings, October 1, 2003.

11. KSB/16/2003, Committee on Culture and the Media proceedings, September 23, 2003.

12. Billig et al. 1988.

13. From the 1989 Hungarian Constitution, the text of which is available on the official website of the Constitutional Court of Hungary, http://www.mkab.hu/. The official English translation of the Hungarian text available on the same website contains a number of omissions and inaccuracies. I have taken the liberty to correct the excerpted parts of the official translation. I should also note that the Constitution cited here was replaced with a Fundamental Law on January 1, 2012.

14. The full text of bills is available at http://www.mkogy.hu/.

15. EMB/31/2003, Committee on Human Rights, Minorities, Civil, and Religious Affairs proceedings, October 7, 2003.

16. Fodor here is calling attention to the Constitutional Court's consistent use of the "clear and present danger" test to determine what types of public expression are to be made subject to legal sanctions.

17. "Alapszabály," retrieved from http://www.szdsz.hu/.

18. In *Nazis in Skokie*, Donald Downs (1985) identified two models of the political community in debates surrounding a proposed neo-Nazi rally in Skokie, Illinois, a village with a sizeable population of Holocaust survivors. Downs argued that supporters of the neo-Nazis' right to march argued according to a "republican virtue model" that prized "intellectual and moral courage, citizen participation in political matters, and the willingness to face the sometimes harsh truths of social and secular existence" (15). Those who were against the march used a "community security model" to build their argument, which "emphasizes the duty of the government and the laws to secure order and justice" (17). A cross-cultural comparison between Downs's models and the Hungarian cultural models discussed in this chapter could yield some interesting differences and similarities between Hungarian and U.S. political and legal discourse.

19. Hall 1988/1989.

20. AIB/38/2003, Constitutional, Judicial, and Standing Orders Committee proceedings, October 1, 2003.

21. Lakoff 2002, 31.

CHAPTER 5

1. Hauser 2002, 99.

2. Carbaugh 2005; Carbaugh and Wolf 1999; Coutu 2000, 2008; Fitch 2003; Griefat and Katriel 1989; Philipsen 1992, 2000; Townsend 2009; Tracy 2002, chap. 2.

3. van Dijk 1984, 106.

4. Carbaugh and Wolf 1999.

5. Agar 1994.

6. See van Dijk 1984, 1992a, 1992b, 1993, 1997; Every and Augoustinos 2007; Fozdar 2008; Machin and Mayr 2007; Seidel 1988.

7. Carbaugh 2007.

8. Schmidt 1996, 15.

9. The coalition was in power between 1994 and 1998 under the leadership of Prime Minister Gyula Horn.

10. Schmidt 1996, 15.

11. In Hungary, the majority of left-wing liberals had opposed legal sanctions against hate speech from the beginning of the controversy.

12. Interview of April 13, 2007. The interviewee wished to remain anonymous.

13. *Ez* (this) points to "hate speech."

14. CEU: the Central European University in Budapest, an international institute of higher education that places a special emphasis on recruiting a diverse student body.

15. Interview of April 12, 2007. The interviewee wished to remain anonymous.

16. Interview of May 16, 2007. The interviewee wished to remain anonymous.

17. *KÓ*, July 26, 2005, 15:36.

18. Seidel 1988, 133.

19. Philipsen 1992, 1997; Philipsen, Coutu, and Covarrubias 2005.

20. Philipsen 2010.

21. Carbaugh 1995.

22. Baxter 1993.

23. Essed 2000.

24. Fairclough 2003, 25.

25. Every and Augoustinos 2007.

26. Pál 2006.

27. Bateson 1973, chap. 1.

28. Intergroup contact, in Bateson's sense, is intercultural contact.

CHAPTER 6

1. "Political action" here means social action with reference to a social issue—more particularly, social action that involves the use of available (communicative, relational, economic, intellectual, etc.) resources for the purpose of expanding one's scope of influence and realizing a set of interests against competing interests.

2. Craig 1989, 2008.

3. Carcasson 2009.

4. Burke 1969.

5. Boromisza-Habashi 2010.

6. Lakoff 2002.

7. Goodall 2010.

8. Billig 1987.

9. Corman, Trethewey, and Goodall 2008.

10. On the critical potential of the ethnographic approach to communication, see Blommaert 2009; Covarrubias 2008; and Hymes 1980.

11. Carbaugh 1989/1990.

12. Ibid., 276.

13. Barber 1984; Gutmann and Thompson 2004; Habermas 1985, chap. 8; Young 2000.

14. Carcasson 2009; Gastil 2006, 2008.

15. Hymes 1972.

16. Miller and Rudnick 2010.

17. Geertz 1973, 12.

18. Quoted in Flyvbjerg 2001.

19. Sanders 2003.

20. Philipsen 2000.

21. Ibid., 225.

22. Carbaugh 1996, xi.

23. Excerpt from Prime Minister Ferenc Gyurcsány's address to the General Assembly of the Hungarian Parliament, April 16, 2007, retrieved from http://mkogy.hu/.

24. "Orbán," 2006.

25. MPs have access to the General Assembly's agenda prior to a day's session.

26. Goodall, Trethewey, and Corman 2008, 5.

27. Hymes 1972.

28. Kaltenbach 2002.

29. "A "cigányozás"" 2006.

30. "Nincs közös nyilatkozat" 2006.

31. "Beszámoló" 2007, 68.

32. Interview of May 2, 2007.

33. "Beszámoló" 2007, 67.

34. Craig 2007.

35. Carbaugh, Boromisza-Habashi, and Ge 2007.

36. Fischer 2003; Throgmorton 1991.

37. Carcasson and Sprain 2009.

38. Burkhalter, Gastil, and Kelshaw 2002, 418.

39. Sanders 1997; Young 1996.

40. Koch 2005, 248.

41. Geertz 1973, 216.

42. Miller and Rudnick 2011.

APPENDIX

1. Marcus 1998.

2. The foundational texts of EC (Carbaugh 1995, 2008; Philipsen 1987, 1992) discuss EC as a research agenda intellectually located in the communication discipline.

3. "Speech community" has a variety of meanings in EC scholarship (see Milburn 2004). Generally speaking, the term points to a group of speakers who share a set of communicative resources (linguistic resources and a system of meanings) and use them to make sense of observable acts of communication. Speech communities need not be geographically contiguous; neither does the concept imply a shared group identity. I use the term "community of speakers" instead of "speech community" to highlight the role of speakers in using, contesting, and transforming shared communicative resources that function as one of the foundations of local social life.

4. Carbaugh 2007.

5. Fitch 2005.

6. Sanders 2005, 2.

7. I conducted a brief Internet search in 2008 to identify other languages besides English and Hungarian whose vocabulary contains literal translations of "hate speech." The search identified Afrikaans (*Haatspraak*), Dutch (*haatdragend taalgebruik, haatuitingen*), French (*discours de haine*), German (*Hassrede, Hasssprache, Sprache des Hasses*), Polish (*mowa nienawiści*), and Serbian (*govor mržnje*).

8. Bauman and Sherzer 1974, 6.

9. Sanders 2005, 6–7.

10. Ibid., 7.

11. Goodwin and Duranti 1992.

12. Fitch 1998.

13. Sherzer 1987, 296.

14. Carbaugh, Gibson, and Milburn 1997, 1.

15. Carbaugh 1991; Philipsen, Coutu, and Covarrubias 2005.

16. Carbaugh 1989; but also see Baxter and Goldsmith 1990; Baxter 1993; Bloch 2003; Bloch and Lemish 2005; Carbaugh 1999; Carbaugh, Berry, and Nurmikari-Berry 2006; Fitch 1998; Garrett 1993; Hall and Noguchi 1995; Hall and Valde 1995; Katriel 2004; Scollo 2004; Wilkins 2005.

17. The Budapest radio station InfoRádió made one radio broadcast available to me free of charge.

18. I stayed in Budapest with my family from January to April 2004, and from January to May 2007.

19. Csepeli and Örkény 2002.

20. "NBH-Évkönyv" 2007.

21. My physical appearance partially explains why I was able to attend these public meetings without gaining attention—I am strikingly Caucasian, with dark blond hair, light skin, and blue eyes.

REFERENCES

"A 'cigányozás' elítélését kéri az ombudsman" [The parliamentary commissioner requests the condemnation of derogatory talk about Gypsies]. 2006. *MŰOSZ*, November 2. http://www.muosz.hu/.

Agar, Michael. 1980. *The professional stranger: An informal introduction to ethnography.* New York: Academic Press.

———. 1994. *Language shock: Understanding the culture of conversation.* New York: William Morrow.

Allport, Gordon W. 1954. *The nature of prejudice.* Reading, Mass.: Addison-Wesley.

"Atrocitásokba torkollott a Tilos Rádió elleni tüntetés: Izraeli zászlót égettek a tüntetők" [Demonstrations against Tilos Rádió lead to atrocities: Demonstrators burn Israeli flag]. 2004. *Index.* January 12. http://index.hu/belfold/tilos5791/.

Austin, John L. 1962. *How to do things with words.* Oxford: Clarendon Press.

"Az ügyészség szerint nem izgatott közösség ellen Barangó" [Chief prosecutor's office says Barangó not guilty of incitement against a community]. 2004. *Index.* February 19. http://index.hu/belfold/tilos0219/.

Babusik, Ferenc. 2005. *Az esélyegyenlőség korlátai Magyarországon* [The limits of equal opportunity in Hungary]. Budapest: L'Harmattan.

Bailey, Frederick G. 1983. *The tactical uses of passion: An essay on power, reason, and reality.* Ithaca: Cornell University Press.

Bálint, Éva. 2000. "Mit tégy a gyűlölet ellen?" [What to do against hatred?]. *Magyar Hírlap Online*, December 8. http://www.magyarhirlap.hu/.

Barany, Zoltan D. 2002. *The East European gypsies: Regime change, marginality, and ethnopolitics.* Cambridge: Cambridge University Press.

Barber, Benjamin R. 1984. *Strong democracy: Participatory politics for a new age.* Berkeley: University of California Press.

Bateson, Gregory. 1973. *Steps to an ecology of mind: Collected essays in anthropology, psychiatry, evolution, and epistemology.* London: Paladin.

Bauman, Richard, and Joel Sherzer. 1974. *Explorations in the ethnography of speaking.* Cambridge: Cambridge University Press.

Baxter, Leslie A. 1993. "'Talking things through' and 'putting it in writing': Two codes of communication in an academic institution." *Journal of Applied Communication Research* 21 (4): 313–26.

Baxter, Leslie A., and Daena Goldsmith. 1990. "Cultural terms for communication events among some American high school adolescents." *Western Journal of Speech Communication* 54 (3): 377–94.

Béres, István, and Özséb Horányi. 1999. *Társadalmi kommunikáció* [Social communication]. Budapest: Osiris.

Bernáth, Gábor, ed. 2000. *Porrajmos: Roma Holocaust túlélők emlékeznek* [Porrajmos: Recollections of Roma Holocaust survivors]. Budapest: Roma Sajtóközpont.

————, ed. 2002. *Kényszermosdatások a cigánytelepeken, 1945–1985* [Forced bathing in Romani settlements, 1945–1985]. Budapest: Roma Sajtóközpont.

————, ed. 2005. *Lakni valahol: Történetek* [To live somewhere: Stories]. Budapest: Roma Sajtóközpont.

"Beszámoló a nemzeti és etnikai kisebbségi jogok országgyűlési biztosának tevékenységéről, 2006 január 1.–december 31." [Report on the activities of the Parliamentary Commissioner of National and Ethnic Minority Rights, January 1–December 31, 2006]. 2007. Budapest: Országgyűlési Biztosok Hivatala. http://www.kisebbsegiombudsman.hu/hir-277-nemzeti-es-etnikai-kisebbsegi-jogok.html.

Bibó, István. 1948/1986. *Válogatott tanulmányok, II kötet, 1945–1949* [Selected essays, vol. 2, 1945–1949]. Budapest: Magvető.

Billig, Michael. 1987. *Arguing and thinking: A rhetorical approach to social psychology.* Cambridge: Cambridge University Press.

Billig, Michael, Susan Condor, Derek Edwards, Mike Gane, David Middleton, and Alan Radley. 1988. *Ideological dilemmas: A social psychology of everyday thinking.* London: Sage.

Bloch, Linda-Renee. 2003. "Who's afraid of being a *freier*? The analysis of communication through a key cultural frame." *Communication Theory* 13 (2): 125–59.

Bloch, Linda-Renee, and Dafna Lemish. 2005. "'I know I'm a *freierit*, but . . .': How a key cultural frame engenders a discourse of inequality." *Journal of Communication* 55 (1): 38–55.

Blommaert, Jan. 2009. "Ethnography and democracy: Hymes's political theory of language." *Text and Talk* 29 (3): 257–76.

Boromisza-Habashi, David. 2010. "How are political concepts 'essentially' contested?" *Language and Communication* 30 (4): 276–84.

Braham, Randolph L. 1981. *The politics of genocide: The Holocaust in Hungary.* New York: Columbia University Press.

"Der Brokerskandal: Symbol ungarischer Zerrissenheit" [The broker scandal: The symbol of Hungary torn apart]. 2004. *Neue Zürcher Zeitung* 29 (February 5): 9.

"Bűnös a 'cukorkás' zászlóégető" [Flag burner "with candy" found guilty]. 2004. *Magyar Hírlap Online*, June 17. http://www.magyarhirlap.hu/.

Burke, Kenneth. 1969. *A rhetoric of motives.* Berkeley: University of California Press.

Burkhalter, Stephanie, John Gastil, and Todd Kelshaw. 2002. "A conceptual definition and theoretical model of public deliberation in small face-to-face groups." *Communication Theory* 12 (4): 398–422.

Butler, Judith. 1997. *Excitable speech: A politics of the performative.* New York: Routledge.

Cameron, Deborah. 1995. *Verbal hygiene.* New York: Routledge.

Carbaugh, Donal. 1988. *Talking American: Cultural discourses on "Donahue."* Norwood, N.J.: Ablex.

————. 1988/1989. "Deep agony: 'Self' vs. 'society' in *Donahue* discourse." *Research on Language and Social Interaction* 22 (1–4): 179–212.

————. 1989. "Fifty terms for talk: A cross-cultural study." In *Language, communication, and culture: Current directions*, ed. Stella Ting-Toomey and Felipe Korzenny, 93–120. Newbury Park, Calif.: Sage.

————. 1989/1990. "The critical voice in the ethnography of communication research." *Research on Language and Social Interaction* 23 (1–4): 261–82.

————. 1990. "Communication rules in *Donahue* discourse." In *Cultural communication and intercultural contact*, ed. Donal Carbaugh, 119–49. Hillsdale, N.J.: Lawrence Erlbaum Associates.

————. 1991. "Communication and cultural interpretation." *Quarterly Journal of Speech* 77 (3): 336–42.

———. 1995. "The ethnographic communication theory of Philipsen and associates." In *Watershed research traditions in human communication theory*, ed. Donald P. Cushman and Branislav Kovačić, 269–97. Albany: State University of New York Press.

———. 1996. *Situating selves: The communication of social identities in American scenes.* Albany: State University of New York Press.

———. 1999. "'Just listen': 'Listening' and landscape among the Blackfeet." *Western Journal of Communication* 63 (3): 250–70.

———. 2005. *Cultures in conversation.* Mahwah, N.J.: Lawrence Erlbaum Associates.

———. 2007. "Cultural discourse analysis: Communication practices and intercultural encounters." *Journal of Intercultural Communication Research* 36 (3): 167–82.

———. 2008. "Ethnography of communication." In *International Encyclopedia of Communication*, 10 vols., ed. Wolfgang Donsbach, 4:1592–98. Malden, Mass.: Blackwell.

Carbaugh, Donal, Michael Berry, and Marjatta Nurmikari-Berry. 2006. "Coding personhood through cultural terms and practices: Silence and quietude as a Finnish 'natural way of being.'" *Journal of Language and Social Psychology* 25 (3): 203–20.

Carbaugh, Donal, David Boromisza-Habashi, and Xinmei Ge. 2006. "Dialogue in cross-cultural perspective: Deciphering communication codes." In *Aspects of intercultural dialogue: Theory, research, applications*, ed. Nancy Aalto and Ewald Reuter, 27–46. Cologne: Saxa Verlag.

Carbaugh, Donal, Timothy A. Gibson, and Trudy Milburn. 1997. "A view of communication and culture: Scenes in an ethnic cultural center and a private college." In *Emerging theories of human communication*, ed. Branislav Kovačić, 1–24. Albany: State University of New York Press.

Carbaugh, Donal, and Karen Wolf. 1999. "Situating rhetoric in cultural discourses." In *Rhetoric in intercultural contexts*, ed. Alberto González and Dolores V. Tanno, 19–30. Thousand Oaks, Calif.: Sage.

Carcasson, Martín. 2009. "Beginning with the end in mind: A call for goal-driven deliberative practice." In *Center for advances in public engagement occasional paper no. 2*. New York: Public Agenda.

Carcasson, Martín, and Leah Sprain. 2009. "Key aspects of the deliberative democracy movement." *Public Sector Digest*, July. https://www.publicsectordigest.com/.

Corman, Steven R., Angela Trethewey, and Harold L. Goodall, Jr. 2008. "A new communication model for the 21st century: From simplistic influence to pragmatic complexity." In *Weapons of mass persuasion: Strategic communication to combat violent extremism*, ed. Steven R. Corman, Angela Trethewey, and Harold L. Goodall, Jr., 151–68. New York: Peter Lang.

Coutu, Lisa M. 2000. "Communication codes of rationality and spirituality in the discourse of and about Robert McNamara's *In Retrospect*." *Research on Language and Social Interaction* 33 (2): 179–211.

———. 2008. "Contested social identity and communication in text and talk about the Vietnam War." *Research on Language and Social Interaction* 41 (4): 387–407.

Covarrubias, Patricia O. 2008. "Masked silence sequences: Hearing discrimination in the college classroom." *Communication, Culture, and Critique* 1 (3): 227–52.

Craig, Robert T. 1989. "Communication as a practical discipline." In *Rethinking communication, vol. 1: Paradigm issues*, ed. Brenda Dervin, Lawrence Grossberg, Barbara J. O'Keefe, and Ellen Wartella, 97–122. Newbury Park, Calif.: Sage.

———. 2007. "Arguments about 'dialogue' in practice and theory." In *Proceedings of the sixth conference of the International Society for the Study of Argumentation*, ed. Frans H. van Eemeren, J. Anthony Blair, Charles A. Willard, and Bart Garssen, 285–90. Amsterdam: Sic Sat.

———. 2008. "Communication as a field and discipline." In *The international encyclopedia of communication, vol.* 2., ed. Wolfgang Donsbach, 675–88. Malden, Mass.: Blackwell.

Craig, Robert T., and Karen Tracy. 2005. "'The issue' in argumentation practice and theory." In *Argumentation in practice*, ed. Frans H. van Eemeren and Peter Houtlosser, 11–28. Amsterdam: John Benjamins.

Csepeli, György, and Antal Örkény, eds. 2002. *Gyűlölet és politika* [Hatred and politics]. Budapest: Friedrich Ebert Alapítvány.

Daróczi, Ágnes, and János Bársony, eds. 2004. *Pharrajimos: Romák sorsa a nácizmus idején, I–II köt.* [Pharrajimos: The fate of Roma during the Nazi era]. Budapest: L'Harmattan.

Dési, János, András Gerő, Tibor Szeszlér, and László Varga. 2004. *Antiszemita közbeszéd Magyarországon, 2002–2003-ban: Jelentés és dokumentáció* [Anti-Semitic discourse in Hungary in 2002–2003: Report and documentation]. Budapest: B'nai B'rith Első Budapesti Közösség.

Downs, Donald A. 1985. *Nazis in Skokie: Freedom, community, and the First Amendment.* Notre Dame: University of Notre Dame Press.

———. 2006. *Restoring free speech and liberty on campus.* New York: Cambridge University Press.

Dzindzisz, Magdaléna. 2001. "Kirekesztés egy kerületi lapban" [Discrimination in a district paper]. *Magyar Hírlap Online*, September 7. http://www.magyarhirlap.hu/.

Eörsi, István. 2004. "Még egyszer a gyűlöletről" [One more time about hatred]. *Élet és Irodalom Online*, November 5. http://www.es.hu/.

Essed, Philomena. 2000. "Beyond antiracism: Diversity, multi-identifications, and sketchy images of new societies." In *The semiotics of racism: Approaches in critical discourse analysis*, ed. Martin Reisigl and Ruth Wodak, 41–61. Vienna: Passagen Verlag.

Every, Danielle, and Martha Augoustinos. 2007. "Constructions of racism in the Australian parliamentary debates on asylum seekers." *Discourse and Society* 18 (4): 411–36.

Fairclough, Norman. 2003. "'Political correctness': The politics of culture and language." *Discourse and Society* 14 (1): 17–28.

Fischer, Frank. 2003. *Reframing public policy: Discursive politics and deliberative practices.* New York: Oxford University Press.

Fitch, Kristine L. 1998. *Speaking relationally: Culture, communication, and interpersonal connection.* New York: Guildford Press.

———. 2003. "Cultural persuadables." *Communication Theory* 13 (1): 100–123.

———. 2005. "Conclusion: Behind the scenes of language and scholarly interaction." In *Handbook of language and social interaction*, ed. Kristine L. Fitch and Robert E. Sanders, 461–82. Mahwah, N.J.: Lawrence Erlbaum Associates.

Flyvbjerg, Bent. 2001. *Making social science matter: Why social inquiry fails and how it can succeed again.* Translated by Steven Sampson. New York: Cambridge University Press.

Fodor, Gábor. 2004. *Gondoljuk újra a polgári radikálisokat* [Let us rethink civic radicals]. Budapest: L'Harmattan.

Fozdar, Farida. 2008. "Duelling discourses, shared weapons: Rhetorical techniques used to challenge racist arguments." *Discourse and Society* 19 (4): 529–47.

Gal, Susan. 1991. "Bartók's funeral: Representations of Europe in Hungarian political rhetoric." *American Ethnologist* 18 (3): 440–58.

———. 1994. "Gender in the post-socialist transition: The abortion debate in Hungary." *East European Politics and Societies* 8 (2): 256–86.

———. 1995. "Linguistic theories and national images in 19th century Hungary." *Pragmatics* 5 (2): 155–66.

Garrett, Mary M. 1993. "Wit, power, and oppositional groups: A case study of 'pure talk.'" *Quarterly Journal of Speech* 79 (3): 303–18.

Gastil, John. 2006. "Deliberation." In *Communication as . . . : Perspectives on theory*, ed. Gregory J. Shepherd, Jeffrey St. John, and Ted Striphas, 164–73. Thousand Oaks, Calif.: Sage.

———. 2008. *Political communication and deliberation*. Thousand Oaks, Calif.: Sage.

Geertz, Clifford. 1973. *The interpretation of cultures*. New York: Basic Books.

———. 1983. *Local knowledge: Further essays in interpretive anthropology*. New York: Basic Books.

Gerő, András. 2004. "A szabadság szemete" [The trash of freedom]. *Élet és Irodalom Online*, October 8. http://www.es.hu/.

———. 2007. "Májusi válasz májusi szavakra: Egy vitacikkről, mely tiszteletet váltott ki belőlem" [A May response to May words: On a polemical article that earned my admiration]. *Magyar Nemzet Online*, May 31. http://www.mno.hu/portal/413639.

Gerő, András, László Varga, and Mátyás Vince. 2001. *Antiszemita közbeszéd Magyarországon 2000-ben* [Anti-Semitic discourse in Hungary in 2001]. Budapest: B'nai B'rith Első Budapesti Közösség.

———. 2002. *Antiszemita közbeszéd Magyarországon 2001-ben: Jelentés és dokumentáció* [Anti-Semitic discourse in Hungary in 2001: Report and documentation]. Budapest: B'nai B'rith Első Budapesti Közösség.

Gombár, Csaba, and Hédi Volosin, eds. 2005. *Két Magyarország?* [Two Hungarys?]. Budapest: Osiris Kiadó–Korridor.

Goodall, Harold L., Jr. 2010. *Counter-narrative: How progressive academics can challenge extremists and promote social justice*. Walnut Creek, Calif.: Left Coast Press.

Goodall, Harold L., Jr., Angela Trethewey, and Steven R. Corman. 2008. "'Strategery': Missed opportunities and the consequences of obsolete strategic communication theory." In *Weapons of mass persuasion: Strategic communication to combat violent extremism*, ed. Steven R. Corman, Angela Trethewey, and Harold L. Goodall, Jr., 3–26. New York: Peter Lang.

Goodwin, Charles, and Alessandro Duranti. 1992. "Rethinking context: An introduction." In *Rethinking context: Language as an interactive phenomenon*, ed. Alessandro Duranti and Charles Goodwin, 1–42. New York: Cambridge University Press.

Goodwin, Jean. 2002. "Designing issues." In *Dialectic and rhetoric: The warp and woof of argumentation analysis*, ed. Frans H. van Eemeren and Peter Houtlosser, 81–96. Dordrecht: Kluwer Academic Publishers.

Griefat, Yousuf, and Tamar Katriel. 1989. "Life demands *musayra*: Communication and culture among Arabs in Israel." *International and Intercultural Communication Annual* 13:121–37.

Gutmann, Amy, and Dennis Thompson. 2004. *Why deliberative democracy?* Princeton: Princeton University Press.

György, Péter. 2004. "Nem értem" [I don't understand]. *Élet és Irodalom Online*, October 22. http://www.es.hu/.

Györgyi, Kálmán. 2003. "A gyűlöletbeszéd és a véleményszabadság jogi értékelése" [A legal assessment of hate speech and freedom of expression]. In *Aktuelle Aspekte des christlich-jüdischen Verhältnisses: A keresztény-zsidó viszony aktuális aspektusai: Nemzetközi szakmai tanácskozás Budapesten, 2003. január, 69–83*. Budapest: Konrad-Adenauer-Stiftung.

Gyurgyák, János. 2001. *A zsidókérdés Magyarországon* [The Jewish question in Hungary]. Budapest: Osiris.

Habermas, Jürgen. 1985. *The theory of communicative action, vol. 2*. Translated by Thomas McCarthy. Boston: Beacon Press.

Hall, Bradford J. 1988/1989. "Norms, action, and alignment: A discursive perspective." *Research on Language and Social Interaction* 22 (1–4): 23–44.

Hall, Bradford J., and Mutsumi Noguchi. 1995. "Engaging in 'kenson': An extended case study of one form of common sense." *Human Relations* 48 (10): 1129–47.

Hall, Bradford J., and Kathleen Valde. 1995. "'Brown nosing' as a cultural resource in American organizational speech." *Research on Language and Social Interaction* 28 (4): 131–50.

Halmai, Gábor. 1994. *A véleményszabadság határai* [The limits of the freedom of opinion]. Budapest: Atlantisz.

Hankiss, Elemér. 2007. "Határhelyzet és átmenet: A kelet-közép-európai átalakulás lehetséges értelmezései" [Liminality and transition: Possible interpretations of transformation in Central Eastern Europe]. *Kétezer* 19 (2): 3–15.

"Harminc napra elhallgattatja az ORTT a Tilost" [ORTT to silence Tilos for thirty days]. 2004. *Index*. January 21. http://index.hu/belfold/ortt0121/.

Harper, Krista. 2006. *Wild capitalism: Environmental activists and post-socialist ecology in Hungary*. Boulder, Colo.: East European Monographs.

———. 2007. "Does everyone suffer alike? Race, class, and place in Hungarian environmentalism." In *Sustainability and communities of place*, ed. Carl A. Maida, 109–26. New York: Berghahn Books.

Hauser, Gerard. A. 2002. *Introduction to rhetorical theory*, 2nd ed. Prospect Heights, Ill.: Waveland Press.

Hegedűs, Lóránt. 2001. "Keresztén Magyar allam!" [Christian Hungarian state!]. *Ebresztő* 3 (3): 1.

"Huszonöt napra elhallgat a Tilos Rádió" [Tilos Rádió to go silent for twenty-five days]. 2005. *Index*. February 24. http://index.hu/belfold/tilos0224/.

Hutchby, Ian. 1996. *Confrontation talk: Arguments, asymmetries, and power on talk radio*. Mahwah, N.J.: Lawrence Erlbaum Associates.

———. 2005. "Conversation analysis and the study of broadcast talk." In *Handbook of language and social interaction*, ed. Kristine L. Fitch and Robert E. Sanders, 347–460. Mahwah, N.J.: Lawrence Erlbaum Associates.

Hymes, Dell. 1962. "The ethnography of speaking." In *Anthropology and human behavior*, ed. Thomas Gladwin, and William C. Sturtevant, 13–53. Washington, D.C.: Anthropological Society of Washington, D.C.

———. 1972. "Models of the interaction of language and social life." In *Directions in sociolinguistics: The ethnography of communication*, ed. John J. Gumperz and Dell Hymes, 35–71. New York: Holt, Rinehart and Winston.

———. 1974. "Ways of speaking." In *Explorations in the ethnography of speaking*, ed. Richard Bauman and Joel Sherzer, 433–51. Cambridge: Cambridge University Press.

———. 1980. *Ethnography in education: Ethnolinguistic essays*. Washington, D.C.: Center for Applied Linguistics.

Kállai, Ernő, and Erika Törzsök, eds. 2000. *Cigánynak lenni Magyarországon: Jelentés 2000* [A Roma's life in Hungary: Report 2000]. Budapest: Európai Összehasonlító Kisebbségkutatások Közalapítvány. http://www.eokik.hu/.

———, eds. 2002. *Cigánynak lenni Magyarországon: Jelentés 2002: A változások, az ígéretek és a várakozások éve* [A Roma's life in Hungary: Report 2002: A year of changes, promises, and expectations]. Budapest: Európai Összehasonlító Kisebbségkutatások Közalapítvány. http://www.eokik.hu/.

———, eds. 2003. *Cigánynak lenni Magyarországon: Jelentés 2003: Látványpolitika és megtorpanás* [A Roma's life in Hungary: Report 2003: Illusory politics and standing still]. Budapest: Európai Összehasonlító Kisebbségkutatások Közalapítvány. http://www.eokik.hu/.

———, eds. 2004. *Cigánynak lenni Magyarországon. Jelentés 2004. Helybenjárás* [A Roma's life in Hungary: Report 2004: Stagnation]. Budapest: Európai Összehasonlító Kisebbségkutatások Közalapítvány. http://www.eokik.hu/.

————, eds. 2006. *Cigánynak lenni Magyarországon: Jelentés 2002–2006: Átszervezések kora* [The age of reorganization. A Roma's life in Hungary: Report 2002–2006]. Budapest: Európai Összehasonlító Kisebbségkutatások Közalapítvány. http://www.eokik.hu/.

Kaltenbach, Jenő. 2002. "'Gyűlöletbeszéd-retorika' a kisebbségi ombudsmanhoz érkezett négy panaszügy tükrében" ["Hate speech rhetoric" in the light of four grievances submitted to the minority ombudsman]. In *Gyűlölet és politika*, ed. György Csepeli and Antal Örkény, 156–65. Budapest: Friedrich Ebert Alapítvány.

Karsai, László, ed. 1992. *Kirekesztők: Antiszemita írások, 1881–1992* [Discriminators: Anti-Semitic publications, 1881–1992]. Budapest: Aura.

Katriel, Tamar. 2004. *Dialogic moments: From soul talks to talk radio in Israeli culture.* Detroit: Wayne State University Press.

Katz, Katalin. 2005. *Visszafojtott emlékezet: A magyarországi romák holokauszttörténetéhez* [Repressed memory: A contribution to the Holocaust history of Hungarian Roma]. Budapest: Pont.

Kemény, István, ed. 1999. *A cigányok Magyarországon* [Gypsies in Hungary]. Budapest: Magyar Tudományos Akadémia.

"Kizárják a Tilos műsorvezetőjét" [Tilos host to be suspended]. 2003. *Index.* December 26. http://index.hu/belfold/tilos031226/.

Koch, Kenneth. 2005. *The collected poems of Kenneth Koch.* New York: Alfred A. Knopf.

Kovács, Zita. 2004. "Szenteste, Tilos Rádió: Kiirtanám az összes keresztényt" [Christmas eve, Tilos Rádió: I would kill off all Christians]. *Magyar Nemzet Online,* December 25. http://www.mno.hu/portal/192794.

Krajczár, Gyula. 2002. "Gyűlöletbeszéd" [Hate speech]. *Népszabadság Online,* January 22. http://nol.hu/cikk/43461/.

Králl, Csaba, ed. 1994. *Holocaust emlékkönyv: A vidéki zsidóság deportálásának 50. évfordulója alkalmából* [Holocaust memorial collection: On the occasion of the 50th anniversary of the deportation of rural Jewry]. Budapest: TEDISZ.

Kubinszky, Judit. 1976. *A politikai antiszemitizmus Magyarországon, 1875–1890* [Political anti-Semitism in Hungary, 1875–1890]. Budapest: Kossuth.

Kulick, Don, and Bambi B. Schieffelin. 2004. "Language socialization." In *Companion to linguistic anthropology,* ed. Alessandro Duranti, 349–68. Malden, Mass.: Blackwell.

Lakoff, George. 2002. *Moral politics: How liberals and conservatives think.* Chicago: Chicago University Press.

Lakoff, Robin T. 2000. *The language war.* Berkeley: University of California Press.

Láng, Zsuzsa. 2011. "A kormányzóerő szűk egy év alatt megbukott" [The government failed within less than a year]. *Népszabadság Online,* April 24. http://nol.hu/.

Machin, David, and Andrea Mayr. 2007. "Antiracism in the British government's model regional newspaper: The 'talking cure.'" *Discourse and Society* 18 (4): 453–77.

Marcus, George E. 1998. *Ethnography through thick and thin.* Princeton: Princeton University Press.

Matsuda, Mari J., Charles R. Lawrence, Richard Delgado, and Kimberle Williams Crenshaw. 1993. *Words that wound: Critical race theory, assaultive speech, and the First Amendment.* Boulder, Colo.: Westview Press.

"Megbeszéljük" [Let's talk about it]. 2004. *Élet és Irodalom Online,* September 10. http://www .es.hu/.

Megyeri, Dávid. 2003. "Gyűlöletkeltés a kormány politikájában" [The arousal of hatred in government politics]. *Magyar Nemzet Online,* November 29. http://www.mno.hu/ portal/187180.

Milburn, Trudy. 2004. "Speech community: Reflections upon communication." *Communication Yearbook* 28:411–41.

Miller, Derek B., and Lisa Rudnick. 2010. "The case for situated theory in modern peacebuilding practice." *Journal of Peacebuilding and Development* 5 (2): 62–74.
———. 2011. "Trying it on for size: Design and international public policy." *Design Issues* 27
(2): 6–16.

NBH-Évkönyv, 2006. 2007. Nemzetbiztonsági Hivatal. http://www.nbh.hu/.

Neményi, Mária, and Júlia Szalai, eds. 2005. *Kisebbségek kisebbsége: A magyarországi cigányok
emberi és politikai jogai* [The minority of minorities: The human and political rights of
Gypsies in Hungary]. Budapest: Új Mandátum.

Németh, László. 1939/1992. "Kisebbségben" [In the minority]. In *A minőség forradalma:
Kisebbségben, vol. 2,* 843–911. Budapest: Püski Kiadó.

Nielsen, Laura Beth. 2004. *License to harass: Law, hierarchy, and offensive public speech.*
Princeton: Princeton University Press.

"Nincs közös nyilatkozat a sajtóban megjelenő 'cigányozásról'" [No joint statement address-
ing derogatory talk about Gypsies in the press]. 2006. *MÚOSZ,* December 27. http://
www.muosz.hu/.

"Orbán: Gyurcsány a demokráciára veszélyt jelentő, beteges hazudozó" [Orbán: Gyurcsány
the compulsive liar a threat to democracy]. 2006. *InfoRádió,* December 13. http://
www.inforadio.hu/hir/belfold/hir-92861.

Pál, Gábor. 2006. "Hate speech: The history of a Hungarian controversy." In *On politics: Rhetoric, discourse, and concepts,* ed. Márton Szabó, 18–21. Budapest: Institute for Political
Science, Hungarian Academy of Sciences. http://e3.hu/pdk/eng/publications/articles.
php.

———. 2011. "Tereket nyitó kulcskategória: A gyűlöletbeszéd fogalma a magyar politikai dis-
kurzusban, 1994–2004" [A key category opening spaces: The concept of hate speech in
Hungarian political discourse]. *Politikatudományi Szemle* 20 (1): 97–118.

Pelle, János. 2001. *A gyűlölet vetése: A zsidótörvények és a magyar közvélemény, 1938–1944*
[Sowing hatred: The Jewish laws and the Hungarian public, 1938–1944]. Budapest:
Európa.

Philipsen, Gerry. 1987. "The prospect for cultural communication." In *Communication theory
from Eastern and Western perspectives,* ed. D. Lawrence Kincaid, 245–54. New York:
Academic Press.

———. 1992. *Speaking culturally: Explorations in social communication.* Albany: State University of New York Press.

———. 1997. "A theory of speech codes." In *Developing communication theories,* ed. Gerry
Philipsen and Terrance L. Albrecht, 119–56. Albany: State University of New York
Press.

———. 2000. "Permission to speak the discourse of difference: A case study." *Research on
Language and Social Interaction* 33 (2): 213–34.

———. 2002. "Cultural communication." In *Handbook of international and intercultural communication,* ed. William B. Gudykunst and Bella Mody, 51–67. Thousand Oaks, Calif.:
Sage.

———. 2010. "Some thoughts on how to approach finding one's feet in unfamiliar cultural
terrain." *Communication Monographs* 77 (2): 160–68.

Philipsen, Gerry, Lisa M. Coutu, and Patricia O. Covarrubias. 2005. "Speech codes theory:
Restatement, revisions, and response to criticisms." In *Theorizing about intercultural
communication,* ed. William B. Gudykunst, 55–68. Thousand Oaks, Calif.: Sage.

Pogonyi, Lajos. 1996. "A gyűlöletbeszéd nem ismeretterjesztés: Csepeli György szociálp-
szichológus a Szabó Albert-perről" [Hate speech does not qualify as the dissemina-
tion of knowledge: Social psychologist György Csepeli on the Albert Szabó lawsuit].
Népszabadság 54, no. 56: 4.

Sanders, Lynn M. 1997. "Against deliberation." *Political Theory* 25 (3): 347–76.

Sanders, Robert E. 2003. "Applying the skills concept to discourse and conversation: The remediation of performance defects in talk-in-interaction." In *Handbook of communication and social interaction skills*, ed. John O. Greene and Brant R. Burleson, 221–56. Mahwah, N.J.: Lawrence Erlbaum Associates.

———. 2005. "Introduction: LSI as a subject matter and as multidisciplinary confederation." In *Handbook of language and social interaction*, ed. Kristine L. Fitch and Robert E. Sanders, 1–14. Mahwah, N.J.: Lawrence Erlbaum Associates.

Scannell, Paddy. 2000. "For-anyone-as-someone structures." *Media, Culture, and Society* 22 (1): 5–24.

Schmidt, Mária. 1996. "Gyűlöletbeszéd, náci beszéd?" [Hate speech, Nazi speech?]. *Népszabadság* 54, no. 97: 15.

Scollo, Michelle S. 2004. "Nonverbal ways of communicating with nature: A cross-case study." In *The environmental communication yearbook, vol. 1*, ed. Susan L. Senecah, 227–49. Mahwah, N.J.: Lawrence Erlbaum Associates.

Seidel, Gill. 1988. "The British New Right's 'enemy within': The antiracists." In *Discourse and discrimination*, ed. Geneva Smitherman-Donaldson and Teun A. van Dijk, 131–43. Detroit: Wayne State University Press.

Sherzer, Joel. 1987. "A discourse-centered approach to language and culture." *American Anthropologist* 89 (2): 295–309.

Smith, Andrew. R., and Fadoua Loudiy. 2005. "Testing the red lines: On the liberalization of speech in Morocco." *Human Rights Quarterly* 27 (3): 1069–1119.

Smitherman-Donaldson, Geneva, and Teun A. van Dijk. 1988. "Introduction: Words that hurt." In *Discourse and discrimination*, ed. Geneva Smitherman-Donaldson and Teun A. van Dijk, 11–22. Detroit: Wayne State University Press.

Spirk, József. 2004. "KereszténWellenes fekáliaöklendezéssel vádolják a Tilost: Közösség elleni izgatás gyanúja" [Tilos charged with anti-Christian feces-retching: Suspicion of incitement against groups]. *Index*. January 6. http://index.hu/belfold/tilos0106/.

Szabó, Márton. 2006a. *Fideszvalóság* [Fidesz-reality]. Budapest: L'Harmattan.

———. 2006b. *Politikai idegen* [Political alien]. Budapest: L'Harmattan.

Tamás, Gáspár Miklós. 2004. "Gerő András téved" [András Gerő is wrong]. *Élet és Irodalom Online*, September 10. http://www.es.hu/.

———. 2007. "Elátkozott magyar ünnepek" [Cursed Hungarian celebrations]. *Népszava Online*, August 18. http://www.nepszava.hu/.

Tannen, Deborah. 1999. *The argument culture: Stopping America's war of words*. New York: Ballantine Books.

Tellér, Gyula. 1996. "A három részmagyarország" [Hungary in three parts]. *Századvég* 1 (1): 52–66.

Throgmorton, James A. 1991. "The rhetorics of policy analysis." *Policy Sciences* 24 (2): 152–79.

"Tilos-ügy: Nem volt izgatás" [Tilos affair: It wasn't incitement]. 2004. *Index*. February 12. http://index.hu/belfold/tilosro212/.

Tomcat. 2004. "Gyűlöletbeszélek" [I am hate-speaking]. May 16. Accessed October 15, 2006. http://blog.tomcatpolo.hu/blog/blog/20040516.html.

Törzsök, Erika, Ildi Paskó, and János Zolnay, eds. 2007. *Cigánynak lenni Magyarországon: Jelentés 2006: A romapolitika kifulladása* [A Roma's life in Hungary: Report 2006: Roma policy runs out of steam]. Budapest: Európai Összehasonlító Kisebbségkutatások Közalapítvány. http://www.eokik.hu/.

———, eds. 2008. *Cigánynak lenni Magyarországon: Jelentés 2007: A gyűlölet célkeresztjében* [A Roma's life in Hungary: Report 2007: In the crosshairs of hatred]. Budapest: Európai Összehasonlító Kisebbségkutatások Közalapítvány. http://www.eokik.hu/.

Townsend, Rebecca M. 2009. "Town meeting as a communication event: Democracy's act sequence." *Research on Language and Social Interaction* 42 (1): 68–89.

Tracy, Karen. 2002. *Everyday talk: Building and reflecting identities.* New York: Guilford Press.

Turner, Victor. 1969. *The ritual process: Structure and anti-structure.* Chicago: Aldine.

———. 1980. "Social dramas and stories about them." *Critical Inquiry* 7 (1): 141–68.

Újhelyi, Zoltán. 2003. "A gyűlölet még nem gyűlöletbeszéd" [Hatred alone is not hate speech]. *Magyar Rádió Online,* September 29. http://www.radio.hu/.

van Dijk, Teun A. 1984. *Prejudice in discourse: An analysis of ethnic prejudice in cognition and conversation.* Amsterdam: John Benjamins.

———. 1992a. "Discourse and the denial of racism." *Discourse and Society* 3 (1): 87–118.

———. 1992b. "Racism and argumentation: Race riot rhetoric in tabloid editorials." In *Argumentation illuminated,* ed. Frans H. van Eemeren, Rob Grootendorst, J. Anthony Blair, and Charles. A. Willard, 243–57. Amsterdam: Sic Sat.

———. 1993. *Elite discourse and racism.* Newbury Park, Calif.: Sage.

———. 1997. "Political discourse and racism: Describing others in Western parliaments." In *The language and politics of exclusion: Others in discourse,* ed. Stephen. H. Riggins, 31–64. Thousands Oaks, Calif.: Sage.

Varga, László. 2004. "A(z egyik) 'háziszerző' belekotyog" [The/One of the "home-grown writer(s)" chimes in]. *Élet és Irodalom Online,* October 15. http://www.es.hu/.

Vértes, Róbert. 1997. *Magyarországi zsidótörvények és rendeletek, 1938–1945* [The Jewish laws and decrees in Hungary, 1938–1945]. Budapest: Polgár.

"Visszaélnek a 'Tégy a gyűlölet ellen' mozgalom nevével" [The name of "Act Against Hatred" movement abused]. 2005. *Népszabadság Online,* May 27. http://www.nol.hu/cikk/363836/.

Walker, Samuel. 1994. *Hate speech: The history of an American controversy.* Lincoln: University of Nebraska Press.

Wilkins, Richard. 2005. "The optimal form: Inadequacies and excessiveness within the *asiallinen* [matter-of-fact] nonverbal style in public and civic settings in Finland." *Journal of Communication* 55 (2): 383–401.

Yankah, Kwesi. 1998. *Free speech in traditional society: The cultural foundations of communication in contemporary Ghana.* Accra: Ghana Universities Press.

Young, Iris M. 1996. "Communication and the other: Beyond deliberative democracy." In *Democracy and difference: Contesting the boundaries of the political,* ed. Seyla Benhabib, 120–35. Princeton: Princeton University Press.

———. 2000. *Inclusion and democracy.* New York: Oxford University Press.

Zelki, János. 2004. "Gerő András tévedése" [András Gerő's lapse]. *Élet és Irodalom Online,* September 17. http://www.es.hu/.

INDEX

Page numbers in *italics* refer to illustrations. Page numbers including "f" or "t" refer to figures and tables, respectively.

Printed in the United States
By Bookmasters